Overcoming Education

Complex Challenges, Difficult People, and the Art of Making a Difference

Brad R. Gustafson

ConnectEDD Publishing
Hanover, Pennsylvania

Copyright © 2024 by Brad R. Gustafson

All rights reserved. No part of this publication may be reproduced, distributed, or transmitted in any form or by any means, including photocopying, recording, or other electronic or mechanical methods, without the prior written permission of the publisher, except in the case of brief quotations embodied in critical reviews and certain other noncommercial uses permitted by copyright law. For permission requests, contact the publisher at: info@connecteddpublishing.com

This publication is available at discount pricing when purchased in quantity for educational purposes, promotions, or fundraisers. For inquiries and details, contact the publisher at: info@connecteddpublishing.com

Published by ConnectEDD Publishing LLC
Hanover, PA
www.connecteddpublishing.com

Cover Design: Kheila Casas
Design adapted from concept created by Afry Harvy

Overcoming Education. —1st ed. Paperback
ISBN 979-8-9911549-1-8

Praise for *Overcoming Education*

Dr. Brad Gustafson has absolutely hit it out of the park with *Overcoming Education*. Brad isn't just an exceptional educational leader; he's a writer who knows how to connect with and inspire readers. As a friend, I've seen firsthand that he truly walks the talk, bringing the same generosity and authenticity to his writing as he does to his everyday work. This book is more than insightful—it's practical and packed with self-reflective moments, real wins, and strategies that keep the reader front and center. My advice…don't skip the introduction—it brilliantly sets the stage for the journey ahead. *Overcoming Education* is a transformational guide that deserves a permanent place on the desks of teachers and school leaders everywhere.

—Allyson Apsey | Educational Leader and Author of *Leading the Whole Teacher*

Dr. Brad Gustafson's *Overcoming Education* is the book to help leaders burn bright, not out. I found myself relating so closely to his words that, at times, it felt like he was writing about me—and directly to me. Written with faith, vulnerability, humility, and a refreshing dose of humor, Brad invites us to rethink the toxic narratives of "just try harder" or "do more." His practical strategies, rich illustrations, and engaging storytelling make the complex challenges of education feel both approachable and solvable as he speaks to those of us stuck in the vicious burnout cycle. Brad reminds us that our struggles don't disqualify us; they prepare us, shaping us to be the leader we are made to be. If you've ever doubted whether real change is possible, Brad's words will reignite your belief that small, intentional steps taken with humility and heart can truly make a difference.

—Zac Bauermaster | Principal, Speaker, and Author of *Leading with a Humble Heart*

Brad Gustafson's *Overcoming Education* is a must-read for educators who are driven to make a difference but feel weighed down by the overwhelming challenges of modern education. With empathy and insight, Gustafson acknowledges the daily struggles educators face—from systemic obstacles to individual setbacks—and offers practical, powerful strategies for overcoming these hurdles. The book stands out for its blend of realism and optimism. Gustafson doesn't ignore the complexity of educational challenges; instead, he validates educators' frustrations and equips them with realistic ways to navigate them. The five fluencies are not just theoretical concepts; they are tangible strategies that can be applied immediately, helping educators move past obstacles and reignite their passion for teaching.

—Jessica Cabeen | Nationally Distinguished Principal, Author, and Speaker

Brad's book arrives just when it's most needed, guiding us through change with wisdom, clarity, and relatability. He invites readers to focus on what truly matters, using a theoretical framework that is refreshingly accessible and practical, offering insights that resonate deeply with educators at every stage. Through his personal experiences and the exercises sprinkled throughout, Brad encourages self-reflection and action, helping educators find purpose and intention in their work. The book's approachable structure allows readers to apply its principles immediately, making it a perfect tool for anyone wanting to make a positive impact. This book can serve as a cornerstone for those striving to build a culture of trust within their organization, encouraging collaboration, open dialogue, and healthy ways to go about this work. It urges us all to pause, reflect, and commit to getting better at getting better. Brad has given us a powerful tool for both personal and collective growth, one that will remain relevant and inspiring for years to come.

—Lynmara Colón | Director of Student Opportunity and Multilingual Services

Brad Gustafson has written an authentic, compassionate, and deeply insightful book that speaks to every educator's challenges and dreams. It's a must-read! In a time when educators are stretched thin, Brad gives us the tools to keep going and to do this work well. As someone who has dedicated my life to education, I find *Overcoming Education* inspiring and indispensable.

—Kelly Croy | Director of Innovation and Instruction for Port Clinton City Schools, Host of *The Wired Educator* Podcast, Author & Speaker

If you have ever met Brad in person or follow him on social media, you understand that he works hard to be positive and engaging in everything he does. In *Overcoming Education*, he breaks down how we can lead during the most complicated of times using five fluencies, which are communication, mindsets, priorities, actions, and who you want to be. All of which will help leaders keep that positive engaging mindset that he models so well.

—Peter DeWitt, EdD | Author/Coach/Facilitator, Instructional Leadership Collective

Overcoming Education is a transformative guide that gets to the very heart of teaching by addressing the underlying challenges educators face within our system. Gustafson's focus on small, manageable actions to overcome complex problems provides invaluable insights and practical strategies that can be implemented immediately. This book is a must-read for anyone in education seeking to make a meaningful difference without becoming overwhelmed. It's a roadmap to effective and sustainable change in our schools through supporting educators and their heartwork.

—Mandy Froehlich | Educator, Author, Mental Health Advocate

Finally! A book that provides practical tools to address the complex challenges of education. Dr. Gustafson does not shy away from hard truths but addresses them in a way that offers hope and a clear path forward, with exercises leaders can implement in their classrooms and schools immediately. Most importantly, in addition to technical skills like communication, he emphasizes the necessary and often-overlooked inner work of the leader, which is where so many leaders rise or fall. If we get our hearts and minds in the right place, everything else starts to crystallize. Agreed!

—Dr. Cindy Hansen | Superintendent, Jasper R-5 School District, Missouri, Adjunct Professor, Bethel University, K-12 EdD Program

Overcoming Education by Dr. Brad Gustafson is a game-changer for anyone aiming to lead with impact. This book makes tackling tough challenges feel doable, breaking down big problems into bite-sized steps and offering straightforward tools for handling tricky situations and people. Dr. Gustafson's 5-Fluency Framework is a flexible, confidence-boosting approach to leadership, and he delivers it all with a perfect mix of storytelling, relatable examples, and practical advice. This book isn't just about problem-solving; it's about rethinking how we face challenges, with an uplifting message that, while education can be overwhelming, making a difference doesn't have to be.

—Michelle Krell | Executive Director, Minnesota Elementary School Principals' Association (MESPA)

Overcoming Education by Dr. Brad Gustafson is a breath of fresh air for educators tackling complex challenges. Through a masterful blend of authenticity, humor, and practical advice, Gustafson shows how small, intentional shifts can lead to big wins in any school setting. His relatable stories and evidence-based insights make this book both engaging and empowering. You'll walk away re-centered and ready to make a difference—without losing your sanity! This is a must-read for anyone who wants to bring hope and heart back into their work.

—Thomas C. Murray | Director of Innovation, Future Ready Schools, 2x Best Selling Author, Washington, D.C.

After learning from Brad Gustafson for the last decade, I knew I'd enjoy reading *Overcoming Education*. What I didn't realize was how impactful this book was going to be not only on me personally, but also professionally. Brad has clearly poured his entire heart into this book and it shows. THIS is the book I wish I would have had when I was in college, or teaching, or even when I started leading a campus. It is filled with countless takeaways and thought-provoking moments. I can't speak highly enough of this incredible resource. Don't just get one copy, because I guarantee you, you'll be sharing yours with someone as soon as you finish it.

—Todd Nesloney | Director of Culture and Strategic Leadership, Texas Elementary Principals and Supervisors Association

If this isn't the best book I have read in years, it is in the conversation. The stories will inspire you. The statistics will shock you. But most of all, *Overcoming Education* will help you walk into school and do the most important work in the world. Gustafson has taken the "To-Do" list of educators and created a "To Be" framework that is accessible and inspiring. It is exceptional in every way and should be required reading for anyone entering the profession, anyone who has lost their way, and anyone who wants to walk into a building with the confidence of a Kindergartner dressed like Batman on Halloween. Gustafson has achieved something many education writers strive for, yet few are able to accomplish–write a book for literally everyone in schools. Everyone. Regardless of role in a school setting...this book is for you. It was written FOR YOU.

—Joe Sanfelippo, PhD | Author, Speaker, and Retired Superintendent

In these disruptive times, Brad Gustafson's book is a beacon of hope for educators. It offers practical strategies to traverse challenges with agility and effectiveness. Focusing on essential leadership fluencies, his well-crafted and researched words will empower educators to embrace change, build strong relationships, and make a lasting impact. This book is a must-read for anyone seeking to transform their practice in ways that focus on the right work.

—Eric Sheninger | Best-Selling Author, Keynote Speaker, and Award-Winning Principal

After thirty years in education, every chapter of this book tugged at my heart. It's easy to feel isolated and lose hope in education, but I genuinely believe that this book would have been a lifesaver in my journey. It has the potential to help every educator or adult working with students develop a stronger version of themselves and their team, creating a better environment for our students to grow and learn. Our family should get the best of us, not what is left of us, and Brad has created skills and strategies to help.

—Curtis Slater | 2018 National Distinguished Principal, Co-Founder, TILL360.Com

Overcoming Education by Dr. Brad Gustafson offers a roadmap for educators, centered around the compelling 'five fluencies' framework: being, mindsets, communication, priorities, and actions. Each fluency offers educators tools to navigate the complexities of teaching, from facing resource constraints to managing overwhelming priorities. Through vivid stories, Dr. Gustafson encourages educators to identify their core purpose and create impact by focusing on fewer, more significant actions, reminiscent of Steve Jobs' focused approach at Apple. Balancing this optimism, however, is the Stockdale Paradox—acknowledging hard truths without losing sight of ultimate success. Gustafson's approach, grounded in collective efficacy, conveys that even small, purpose-driven actions can ripple through our classrooms and beyond. This book resonates powerfully as both a guide and an earnest call to action for those committed to meaningful, sustainable change in education.

—Errol St. Clair Smith, Executive Producer, BAM Education Radio Network

Overcoming Education is a beacon for educators who are caught in the struggle between big challenges and limited support. It takes a brutally honest look at the realities of our profession—burnout, stress, and the feeling that we're all just supposed to "try harder." But it also offers something invaluable: hope through practical strategies and real solutions. With a thoughtful, down-to-earth style, Dr. Gustafson speaks directly to those of us in the trenches, reminding us that overcoming isn't about monumental change; it's about small, focused actions that we can control. This book is not only a guide for solving the complex challenges we face but also a companion that understands just how deeply we care. If you've ever felt overwhelmed but still believe in the power of education to change lives, you need to read this.

—Amber Teamann | Executive Director of Tech & Innovation

Brad Gustafson's *Overcoming Education* isn't just another book on educational leadership—it's a refreshing take on how to actually make change. Brad Gustafson's insights on navigating challenges are spot-on. He doesn't just offer platitudes; he provides concrete, actionable strategies, all while keeping you engaged with his relatable stories and sense of humor. Most importantly, he reminds us to focus on who we want to be as educators, a subtle shift that can make a world of difference. I highly recommend this book for anyone looking to make an impact in our field.

—Sarah Thomas, PhD | CEO, EduMatch

In *Overcoming Education*, Brad Gustafson blends intriguing research, powerful data, inspiring stories, and practical exercises to guide educators. This book, written in a conversational voice with frequent humor, is filled with easy-to-follow activities for teachers and their teams. Brad Gustafson's style and empathy will motivate leaders to not only overcome challenges of teaching, but also make a difference and create joy.

—Jeff Wells | High School Teacher and Coach, Boone, Iowa

Dedication

For every educator navigating complex challenges and change.
I hope this book supports you on your journey.

Table of Contents

Introduction: *Big Dreams, Broken Records, and Bay Leaves* 1
    A Dangerous Idea.. 1
    The Struggle is Real 2
    How Did We Get Here? 5
    My Mission 7
    Small and Solvable 8
    Find Your Focus 10
    Validating Doubt and Disbelief 13
    How to Make a Difference 15
    Your First Win 18
    My Promise to You... 19

Chapter 1: *Drilling Down* 21
    The Advice of Blue Scuti....................................... 21
    The Problem is Complex....................................... 23
    How People Try to Solve Problems........................ 24
    Priority-Selection (Exercise).................................. 26
    Deconstructing Innovation 28
    What About Relationships?! 30
    The Jam Stand Experiment................................... 31
    Another Win.. 32
    Reduction is Essential 33
    The 5-Fluency Framework 35

    The Best Movies Ever Made 37
    One More Thing We Need to Invest In 40
    Validating Doubt and Disbelief 42
    The Heart of the Matter 44

Chapter 2: *The Power of "Who You Want to Be"* 47
    The Banyan Tree 48
    Comparing with Intention 49
    "Who Do You Want to Be?" on the Continuum (Exercise) 50
    Crafting "Who You Want to Be" (Exercise) 53
    Isabella Baumfree 55
    Name Your Challenges (Exercise) 56
    Naming, Blaming, and Reframing 58
    Reframe with Caution 60
    Moving from "What" to "Who" 62
    How to Lead with "Who" 65
    Applying the Framework (Exercise) 66
    Validating Doubt and Disbelief 69
    Growing Forward 70

Chapter 3: *Mindsets—How to Whisper with More Wolves* 71
    The Things People Think 71
    Validating Doubt and Disbelief 73
    A Cosmic Catapult 74
    Mental Postures 76
    Mindsets as Actions of Thought 78
    The Power of Thinking Differently 80
    The Wolves We Befriend 81
    Anna Muzychuk 83
    Exploring Mindsets (Exercise) 85
    The Daily Aspiration 88
    Poisoned Pawns 89

TABLE OF CONTENTS

    No More Flat Tires 91
    The Pack 93

**Chapter 4: Communication—How to Speak the
Language of Connection** **95**
    Lost in Translation. 95
    Quick-Response (Exercise). 97
    Communication as an Act of Connection. 99
    Connect Vertically 101
    Connect Horizontally 103
    Connect Diagonally 106
    Validating Doubt and Disbelief 109
    Frequencies, Feelings, and Failing to Connect 109
    The Great Mini-Cinnamon Roll Conflict. 111
    How to Create Connection. 113
    Think, Know, and Be (Exercise) 115
    The Language of Connection 117

Chapter 5: Priorities—Moving Beyond Common Ground **119**
    The Forest Man 119
    Jadav Payeng Worked Alone. 130
    Priority Pulse Check (Exercise) 122
    People, Priorities, and Blockbuster Movies about
        Shark Attacks. 124
    A Brief History of Common Ground 127
    The Tyranny of Familiar 128
    Beyond Common Ground. 130
    The Places People Frequent 131
    The Backfire Effect. 135
    Three Strategies in One. 137
    Hope for Tomorrow. 138
    Validating Doubt and Disbelief 140
    Moving Forward. 140

Chapter 6: *Actions—Subtle Shifts Can Change Everything* **143**
    The Power of Subtle Shifts 143
    Less is Smart 145
    The One Thing Most People Aren't 147
    Habit Stacking (Exercise) 148
    Validating Doubt and Disbelief 150
    Seeing the Connection 151
    The Stockdale Paradox 153
    Creating Constellations 155
    Becoming "O.P." and "Broken" 157
    The Almost Invisible Triangle 159
    Social Proof 162
    Your Green Light 163

Chapter 7: *Finishing Strong* **165**
    The Return of Blue Scuti 166
    The Art of Reduction 167
    Sympathetic Resonance 169
    The Candy Cane 171
    The Enduring Authority of Small 173
    Micromanaging vs. Making Micro-Differences 175
    Validating Doubt and Disbelief 177
    Be Confident—You Can Do This! 178

Acknowledgment **181**

Notes **185**

Integrity of Research and Writing **199**

About the Author **201**

More from ConnectEDD Publishing **203**

I tell you the truth, if you have faith the size of a mustard seed, you will say to this mountain, "Move from here to there," and it will move. Nothing will be impossible for you.

Matthew 17:20-21

INTRODUCTION

Big Dreams, Broken Records, and Bay Leaves

There's no doubt in my mind you're here to overcome. Not just because you're diving into this book. But because you're the kind of person who is *all in* on learning–starting with the Introduction. I'm committed to making this more than worth your time. By the end of this Introduction, we'll be celebrating two important wins together. So, let's dive in and make your victory lap happen!

A Dangerous Idea

My parents divorced when I was in the 3rd grade. After that, my dad had visitation time with my sister and me on Mondays, Wednesdays, and every other weekend. Therefore, we grew up on a semi-regular diet of frozen pizza, chicken nuggets, and sci-fi.

Spending time with dad produced some important life lessons. Like, when it comes to frozen food, "not bad" isn't necessarily good. But Dad's affinity for outer-space adventures taught us something, too. Whether it was *Star Wars* or *Star Trek*, my sister and I consistently saw how one person, team, or Rebel Force could overcome impossible odds.

The message always seemed to be that people can conquer anything—as long as they dream big enough, put in the effort, or have the right amount of lightsaber training. But this cultural mindset isn't necessarily helping educators.

The idea that we just need to try harder or work longer hours to overcome our challenges is dangerous. It flows from a fundamentally flawed mindset. Yet, it is often a go-to strategy.

Trying harder is one of the mental leaps our brains make without us even having to think about it. In psychology, these mental shortcuts are called heuristics.[1] Our brains automatically create and use them to free up bandwidth and enhance efficiency.

However, they can also work against us. Which is part of the reason many of us believe our biggest problems require big solutions. There's a proportionality bias at work that's preventing us from accessing our best thinking.[2]

There are other mind traps and mantras that might be working against us as well. Innocent phrases like, "We're all in this together" and "Teamwork makes the dream work" may be true. But they're also two of the greatest oversimplifications in education.

I'm not saying teamwork isn't important. But reinforcing a culture where things like "being in it together" and "just trying harder" are the primary solutions being offered is not necessarily helpful. Not while so many educators are feeling overworked, under-supported, and needing to ask for donations just so students can blow their noses.

The Struggle is Real

Many educators are struggling. We're struggling with student mental health, a lack of time and support, and the feeling that this work is not sustainable.[3] Not to mention student discipline, chronic absenteeism, school safety, and the proliferation of social media.

Any of these things alone would be tricky. But when they all come to a head in the same space where you're trying to make a difference—they can become overwhelming. Is it any wonder why so many of us go home from work unable to make simple decisions about what's for dinner?

To make things even more complex, disparities in achievement, opportunity, and an increasingly divisive climate demand our attention. They can make teaching, leadership, and parent phone calls feel more like walking on eggshells than anything else. Yet, we continue to hear familiar refrains like…

> Change takes time.
> Go slow to go fast.
> Patience is a virtue.
> This is a marathon not a sprint.
> Rome wasn't built in a day.*

While I appreciate the intent of these phrases, I don't think we can wait indefinitely for real solutions to complex challenges. Time is a luxury we do not have.

33%

In a recent RAND survey, 33% of adults working outside education are "often or always" stressed by work.[5] But here's the catch—and I

---

* *Historians estimate the total time it took to build Rome to be 1,229 years. This spans the time from its founding in 753 B.C. to its collapse in 476 A.D. when its borders were breached by Germanic tribes. Some argue it took closer to 800 years to build Rome because the city's population maxed out between half a million to a million people in the second century A.D. Either way, comparing anything in education to how long it took to build Rome isn't practical.[4]*

admit I buried the lead here—while 33% of other working adults said work is "often or always stressful," almost 80% of superintendents said they were "often or always" stressed.[6]

55%

Teachers are struggling, too. The National Education Association reported a whopping 55% of its members are considering leaving the profession…this is up from 37% in a previous survey.[7]

A survey conducted by the National Association of Secondary School Principals found the stress level of school administrators is also high. Half were looking to change careers or retire.[8,9] A California Case Study found principals working in high-poverty urban schools are 50 percent more likely to leave than those in a low-poverty suburban schools.[10]

98%

If you find yourself struggling, but still believe you can make a difference, you're not alone. 98% of people believe a good teacher can change the trajectory of a student's life.[11] This is a massive number! I'm also assuming the other 2% misread the survey question.

> **This is still the profession that transforms lives. We know we make a difference. Almost everyone outside education believes we make a difference, too. However, waiting on them to provide the solutions and support you need to make this work more manageable isn't working out very well. Therefore, this is a book about empowering you and your team.**

BIG DREAMS, BROKEN RECORDS, AND BAY LEAVES

How Did We Get Here?

On September 12, 1962, President John F. Kennedy shared a historic message at Rice Stadium.[12] The message is known as his "We choose to go to the moon" speech. President Kennedy listed several other feats during that speech, including climbing the highest mountains and flying across the Atlantic.[13] But landing a rocket on the moon was an idea born in another stratosphere. Especially when considering America wasn't even winning the space race at that time.

President Kennedy seemed to acknowledge the impossibility of it all when he said, "We choose to go to the moon in this decade and do the other things not because they are easy, but because they are hard."[12] And like clockwork, less than eight years after President Kennedy inspired a nation to pursue the impossible, Commander Neil Armstrong and Buzz Aldrin set foot on the moon. However, the context and conditions in which they achieved this big dream are drastically different from the reality we're working in today.

Getting the Apollo 11 crew to fly 240,000 miles to the moon required a singularity of purpose involving thousands of companies from every sector.[14] It was a mobilization of resources at a scale most of us can't fathom. And the numbers[14] don't lie:

$180,000,000,000.00

The mission had a massive budget. In the 1960's, NASA's budget was more than 4 percent of the federal budget. In today's dollars, the overall price tag for Apollo would be around 180 billion dollars.

20,000

The human resources and cross-sector collaboration of the Apollo program involved 20,000 companies and 400,000 people. This included businesses, colleges, and other agencies working together to propel the program and vision forward.

"One"

When Neil Armstrong took his first step on the moon and declared, "That's one small step for man, one giant leap for mankind" he was far from alone.[14] At that moment, he might have been the most supported person in the galaxy. Literally.

And the rest, they say, is history. Or is it?! Some of the same limitless thinking is alive and well in education–for good reason. As educators, we are no strangers to having a noble purpose, bold vision, and needing to blaze new trails in order to achieve our goals. But there are some dramatic differences between the Apollo program and you (see figure 0.1).

4 DIFFERENCES BETWEEN THE APOLLO PROGRAM AND YOU

1. YOU DON'T HAVE A DECADE TO FIGURE OUT HOW TO MEET THE NEEDS OF YOUR STUDENTS
2. YOUR BUDGET ISN'T $180,000,000,000.00
3. YOU DON'T HAVE 400,000 PEOPLE DIRECTLY SUPPORTING YOUR SUCCESS
4. YOU'RE PROBABLY NOT THE SINGLE-MOST SUPPORTED PERSON IN THE GALAXY

Figure 0.1: Differences between the Apollo program and you

Students don't have a decade to learn the skills they need to be successful in whatever grade-level they are in. And the budgets we are working with can make finding a working dry-erase marker feel like a victory. The level of tangible support you receive from other sectors is also different. All this adds up to you *not* being the single-most supported person in the galaxy.

My Mission

Early in the development of this book, friends would ask me who I was writing for. They were noticing how I would use the words "educator" and "leader" interchangeably when talking about the book. So I want to clarify that for you right now.

This book is for educators who want to make a difference but are struggling with complex challenges. Challenges that seem to find their way to us regardless of our official job titles. Therefore, my decision to use the words *educator* and *leader* interchangeably is intentional.

This book is for you if you're an educator. (Because I think you're a leader, too). Regardless of your role, students are impacted by how you show up. Your team notices how you treat people. Families are looking to you to set the standard—even if they sometimes struggle to follow the standard.

You are a leader. And I'm going to do everything I can to help you overcome the things holding you back from making a difference. I'm not going to tell you what you should think, do, or say when other people are making your job difficult. I may share some suggestions along the way. But everything in this book is an invitation. Which means that your strengths and experiences are needed as we embark on the journey ahead.

As a practicing principal working alongside an incredible team, I see how hard educators are working. But I'm also keenly aware how hard some of the challenges we're facing are. And some of these challenges are not going well for everyone. I've noticed similar themes in my role as a speaker, author, and leadership consultant.

Educators want to make a difference. But many of us are experiencing a slow and silent decline. It wasn't long ago that I was one of them. I would head home from work each day overwhelmed by the stress of it all. Seeing our students and staff struggling was wrecking me. When I was home, I wasn't really home. My mind was either replaying the day's challenges, thinking about students' mental health needs, or worried about how we'd survive the following day. It wasn't a good situation. I started having panic attacks at night. For more than a year, I did everything I could to overcome it all.

You might question why somebody who was struggling to navigate his job should be trusted to help you and your team make a difference. This is a fair question. However, I've come to realize the complex challenges our team was working through (and continue to work through) don't disqualify me from trying to help others. They might actually make me a little more equipped to understand the challenges you and your team are up against. And how to overcome them.

> Whether you're leading transformational change or just trying to survive, I'm committed to helping you and your team overcome.

Small and Solvable

Overcoming is a skill. Therefore, it can be learned. But you must be able to see the small and solvable parts of larger problems.

Tom Brady wasn't supposed to be successful in college. Not by a long shot. But he eventually won seven Super Bowl championships as a quarterback in the National Football League.[15] Regardless of how you feel about the New England Patriots, or Brady himself, his story offers us some social proof that would be easy to miss—if you weren't looking for it. As a college quarterback at Michigan, Brady was 7th on the depth chart.[16] To put this in educational terms, Brady was on the "do not call" sub list (see figure 0.2).

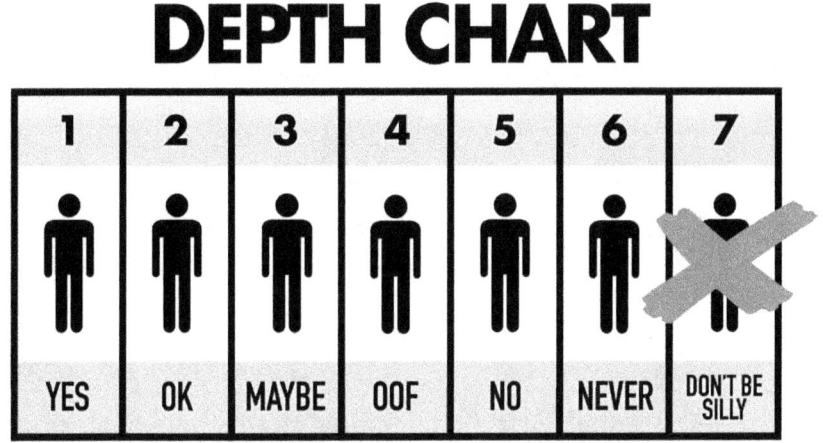

Figure 0.2: Depth chart

At one point in college, Brady was so frustrated with being a 7th-string backup that he met with Greg Harden, a counselor who was working in Michigan's athletic department.[16] As the story goes, Brady complained about only getting three reps at each practice. Harden replied, "Three reps is better than zero," and encouraged him to make the most of what he was getting.

From that point on, Brady trained his body and mind to do just that. He brought a focus to each of his three reps that's typically reserved for the Super Bowl—not the leftover scraps of a college football practice. It wasn't long before his three reps became more. And more. With each increase in practice time, Brady's impact on his team grew. He eventually earned the starting quarterback position at Michigan, making him #1 on the depth chart.

Your challenges are different from those that Tom Brady was facing. As an educator, you've probably been given *more* reps, daily responsibilities, and online training modules than most people could balance in a month. But there is something in Brady's story that you will want to pay attention to.

The perspective Tom Brady adopted from his counselor and coaches was important. And it can help you overcome your brain's tendency to look for bigger solutions, more control, or additional playing time.

> The lesson is, *small things carry authority over big problems.*

Find Your Focus

Overcoming is a skill. But if you don't focus on what's essential, it's easy to become overwhelmed by everything else.

Dr. Gladys West grew up in Dinwiddie County, Virginia.[17] She had big dreams from an early age. But her dreams did not involve working in the fields of her family's farm. So she focused on education. And math.

Dr. West walked three miles every day to get to a one-room schoolhouse. But she didn't stop there. She was named Valedictorian of her high school class and earned a scholarship to Virginia State College. After that, she became a teacher and went on to study advanced mathematics in graduate school, eventually earning a PhD from Virginia Tech.

In 1956, Dr. West became only the second African American woman to work at the Naval Proving Ground.[18] Over the next four decades, she took part in award-winning studies and became project manager for the team that developed the first satellite capable of monitoring oceans. In 2018, she was inducted into the US Air Force Hall of Fame.

Dr. West's life is marked by excellence and focus. From a young age, she saw education as a transformational force. And that's exactly what it became. But not just to her. Dr. West's intense focus on education and mathematics led to the development of what we now know as Global Positioning Systems (GPS),[17] a technology that's become an integral part of millions and millions of lives. Focus matters.

The lesson becomes, *small things carry authority over big problems. But not every small thing. It's important to focus on the small things that are essential to making a difference.*

The remainder of this book will focus on helping you overcome your leadership challenges through a focus on five essential elements of practice. I call the elements *fluencies*. Because the more you practice using them together, the more natural they become. Similar to how Dr. West focused on education *and* math–a transformative combination she tapped into throughout her life.

The fluencies have underpinned my work with leaders, schools, and organizations around the country. They are informed by research, grounded in psychology, and connected to data gleaned from several different sectors. The five essential fluencies are: *Communication, Mindsets, Priorities, Actions,* and *Who You Want to Be*. Together, the fluencies form a framework that can help us navigate complex challenges.

I'm committed to helping you see the fluencies and framework within the larger challenges you and your team are working on–as vividly as a Heads-Up Display (HUD) might appear on the windshield of a vehicle (see figure 0.3). And similar to how Dr. Gladys West's pioneering work with GPS is helping millions of us navigate the world. The fluencies can guide us through complex challenges with confidence.

I'll share more about how you and your team can actually use the five essential fluencies in the pages that follow. But for right now, you'll want to remember two things:

Figure 0.3: Heads-up display of framework

1. Focusing on one fluency has the potential to change your practice.
2. Accessing different combinations of the fluencies can change everything.

The fluencies we will focus on have been distilled from years of research, practices that have proven effective time and time again, and work with educators and organizations across the country–including the school where I get to work each day. However, they are not the only way to make a difference. I'm not naive enough to presume there's only one pathway or approach to overcoming.

Make the journey your own. Embrace the times when you disagree with me. Notice when your instincts tell you that you know your students and team better than I do. It's true. You're right. I'm here to help, but I can't do that without your expertise and knowledge.

Validating Doubt and Disbelief

Have you ever read something you weren't totally sure about? Like maybe even the Introduction to this book?! As I just mentioned, your doubts are welcome here. I'll pause every chapter to create a space for a question or two that you might be wrestling with. For example…

You might be wondering:
"What if I struggle with self-doubt?"

This is a secret fear that bubbles up inside me, too. I'm a chronic overthinker. Much of my obsessing revolves around replaying things I could've (or should've) said differently during conversations and meetings. So here's what I'll say to you–I *feel* you.

Reading this book will not eliminate your self-doubt, just like writing it didn't erase mine. But it will increase your capacity to see the small and meaningful things you and your team can do. It will also provide you with the research, receipts, and social proof so you can see how people are successfully applying what you're reading. And there is confidence to be gained in that.

Or…
"I'm not doubting myself—I'm doubting the author!
What makes him credible?"

Dang. You had to go there?! (Don't worry—I would, too!) I struggle to answer this because I'm much more comfortable acknowledging my shortcomings than trying to convince people I don't have them. So let's start there.

I'm passionate about eating at chain restaurants* that any respectable foodie would avoid. I've been accused of being tone deaf, too. Yet, I love to belt out random songs for no apparent reason. Which means I'm not always pleasant to be around.

I have a hard time picking up my kids' prescriptions at the pharmacy – mostly because of that pesky question they always ask about my kids' dates-of-birth. (And not having the birthdates of my kids memorized automatically removes me from any father-of-the-year consideration.)

On a very serious note, nearly 30% of the students I get to work with are not proficient in reading and math—this is not acceptable to me or anyone I know. It also proves you're reading a book written by somebody who has a lot to learn. Again, I'm not sharing this statistic lightly.

With all this said, there's a chance you were hoping to learn a little more than just *"Don't take restaurant recommendations from this guy."* Especially since we have such an important journey ahead. So here's what I'll share...

You're reading a book written by an educator who understands the importance of the people around him. I believe our team is everything. We sharpen each other. We challenge each other. We elevate and enhance everything that matters in our school. This doesn't mean we always agree. But it does mean that I get to work with some of the most talented professionals and top-notch people I've ever met.

Now that you have me fired up, there's one more thing you should know about our team. There's a chance we're struggling with some of the same (or similar) challenges you and your team are facing. We're trying to navigate innovation, important instructional shifts, and what in the world to make of AI. But there are also days when we're just trying to survive. The point is, when I refer to *complex challenges*, I'm not only talking about navigating technology shifts and change. I'm also

---

* *I don't care what any foodie says. I highly recommend the boneless wings and seasoned fries at Applebees. So good!*

talking about trying to create the conditions where the basic needs of everyone in school (including educators!) are prioritized.

How to Make a Difference

If *overcoming* is a skill, making a difference is an art. Understanding this art will help you hit the ground running instead of spinning your tires. Kate Maggetti knows a thing or two about speed. In September of 2023, Kate and her university teammates gathered at a military airfield in Dübendorf, Switzerland.[19] They were hoping to break the record for the time it takes an electronic vehicle to travel from 0 to 60mph. And break it they did! It only took Maggetti's car 40 feet (12.3 meters) of track and less than a second to reach 60 mph.*

Beating the record was not an accident. Maggetti's team excelled on a scale so small, Tom Brady would have been jealous. And the math involved would have had Dr. Gladys West giving out high-fives.

Maggetti's vehicle was crafted from a carbon fiber and aluminum honeycomb, making it incredibly light. To reduce the risk of a spin-out at the starting line, her team designed a vacuum system to suction the car and its tires to the track. And instead of relying on one larger engine, the team leveraged four smaller, in-wheel motors that generated 326 horsepower.[20] This combination helped them trim the milliseconds needed to beat the record.

Thinking about the same things in the same way doesn't get transformational results. Sometimes making a difference requires you to see familiar things differently. Which is exactly why I'm also going to help you and your team see each fluency in a nuanced way as we progress through the chapters ahead (see figure 0.4).

---

* *The record Kate and her team broke was set on the same airfield that students from the University of Stuttgart broke the record on in 2022. The old record was 1.461 seconds – making Kate's time a whopping 65% faster.*[19]

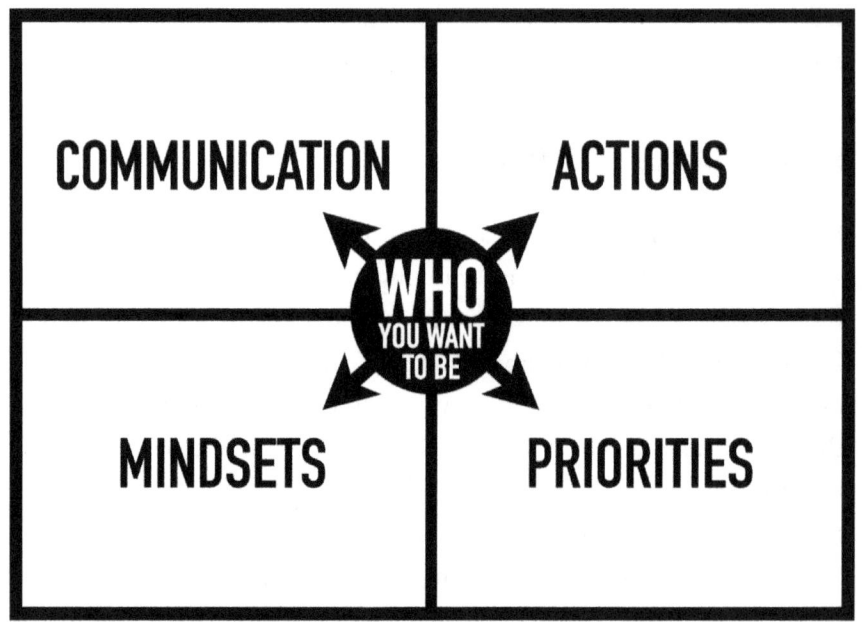

Figure 0.4: The 5-Fluency Framework

In addition to seeing each individual fluency differently, I will also show you how to connect the fluencies. For example, we'll explore how focusing on the vertical connection between Mindsets and Communication creates authenticity (see figure 0.5). And how strengthening the horizontal connection between your Communication and Actions builds trust (also in figure 0.5).

But before we dive into that wizardry, you should know that the fluency in the center of the framework influences everything. Which is why I've unofficially dubbed it a super-fluency. Here's an anecdote that will shed some light on what I mean.

BIG DREAMS, BROKEN RECORDS, AND BAY LEAVES

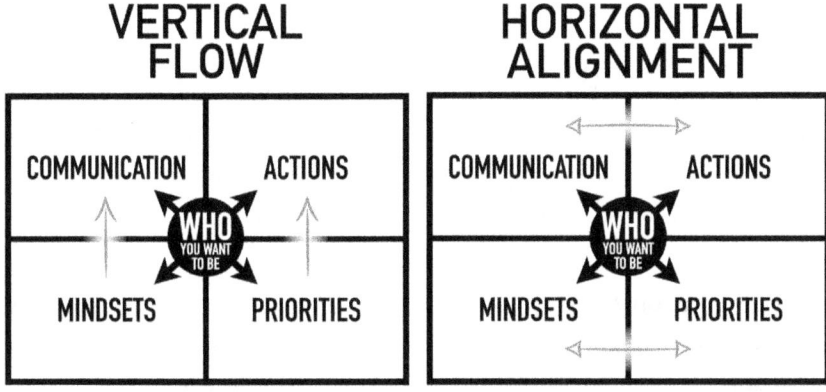

Figure 0.5: Connect the fluencies to enhance your leadership

The brilliant Dr. John Spencer recently reflected on a conversation he had with a chef.[21] At one point in their conversation, John asked, "So, bay leaves?!" After that, John expanded on his question and said, "Do they even have a point? You can't taste them. You have to take them out. They seem to get in the way."

The chef responded by shaking his head and saying, "Nah, it's the opposite…they're the invisible heroes of culinary arts. Bay leaves won't give you a distinct flavor. They don't stand out. It can be so subtle you don't even detect it. But what they do is offer depth. They're a small thing that makes a big difference. They're working behind the scenes to amplify everything else. Trust me…they're a big deal."

The dot in the center of the framework is the bay leaf of education. *Who You Want to Be* flavors everything. But this doesn't necessarily happen on its own. Therefore, the arrows coming out from the dot serve as a visual reminder. Before you think about any of the other fluencies, I'm going to show you how to access *Who you want to be*—so that your aspirational thinking informs and transforms whatever you choose for your next steps.

Your First Win

When it comes to helping you and your team overcome, I am not messing around. This is one reason we're going to stop and celebrate you (right now!). You've already accomplished two important things—and you haven't even finished the Introduction to this book.

First, you understand many people in our profession are struggling and you have some of the research to back it up. These are real numbers representing real people. Leaders like you and me. So, your first victory is knowing there's NOTHING wrong with you. **Everybody is struggling with something.**

Second, you're aware of the brain's tendency to seek out bigger solutions when facing complex challenges. Which means you are better positioned to look for the small and solvable aspects of complex challenges. Sometimes I refer to this as *seeing the smalvable*. By the end of this book, I hope this is one of your Jedi skills—just like those legendary figures learned to master their craft through focus and intention.

You're also aware of a few people who overcame incredible odds by thinking on a different scale. Tom Brady took the paltry three plays he was given each practice and turned those into seven Super Bowl rings. Dr. Gladys West focused on two small and mighty things to transform her life—and many of our lives as well. Kate Maggetti's team applied innovative thinking on a micro scale in order to reach unprecedented speeds.

These stories represent a sliver of the social proof we'll be diving into together, using examples from education and countless other sectors. But the best news is that you're part of the story. Because the strategies and framework you take away from reading can be applied to the challenges you and your team are facing.

> You can overcome, too!

My Promise to You

Waiting on large-scale solutions and support worked for the Apollo 11 crew. But our mission is different. Therefore, we need to think on a different scale. I haven't given up hope that meaningful change and system-level support is coming. However, while we're waiting on these things, it's important to maximize the difference we can make today.

My promise is simple. After reading this book, you will be able to see the small and solvable aspects of complex challenges. Because when you and your team can see small things in your control, you can make a difference—without having to sacrifice your personal life, precious time, or sanity.

To be clear, we're not going to focus on anything and everything small. We're going to practice seeing and leveraging five essential fluencies which represent the essential aspects of practice hidden inside virtually every complex challenge you'll ever encounter. (You'll learn why this is such a big deal in the chapters ahead.)

As a small disclaimer, you and your team will still experience challenges. You just will. But I suspect you already knew that. I want to help you lean into those challenges with humble confidence. But I also want to help you become a living example of this book's core message:

> Education can be overwhelming. But making a difference doesn't have to be.

CHAPTER 1

Drilling Down

Most people approach their problems with a few specific go-to strategies. But what if some of our favorite ways of solving problems are actually working against us. (They are!)

In this chapter, I'll make the case for the core message of this book: **Education can be overwhelming. But making a difference doesn't have to be.**

I'll share social proof from several different sectors—including science, technology, and the often-overlooked world of jam and jelly sales—so that you can be confident the framework and strategies in this book can help you and your team make a difference, too.

The Advice of Blue Scuti

Growing up, you could usually find me outside. Playing kickball, building forts, or doing stuff that was not smart on my bike. Every day was an adventure. But there was one adventure my mom wasn't a fan of. And it involved an Atari 2600. Which meant playing video games was not something you'd find me doing very often. However, all bets were off when Mom was teaching summer school. That's when my world was reduced to a gaming console, our basement, and my babysitter–Ryan.

OVERCOMING EDUCATION

I don't want to misrepresent myself (or Ryan). But I was *made* to play Atari football. And Ryan was not. One time the game went so badly for Ryan that he walked upstairs and proceeded to retire from babysitting me. In Ryan's defense, I was not the most gracious winner when I was eight years old.

I recently read a story that transported me back in time to my childhood basement. On December 21, 2023, a 13-year-old who goes by the screen name "Blue Scuti," beat Tetris. Technically, he did more than just beat the game—he broke it.[22] After reaching level 157, Blue Scuti got to the "kill screen." In video-gaming lore, a kill screen is the point in a game when somebody plays so well they trip up the computer code—similar to breaking a scoreboard.[23]

Prior to Blue Scuti's accomplishment, the only other time a Tetris kill screen had been reached was by an AI-powered robot.*

In an interview after the game, Blue Scuti said, "If you try hard enough and set your mind to something…you will get it." The advice he shared was inspiring. But what if it isn't exactly true—at least not for you and me?!

> **In video games, you can dedicate yourself to getting a high score or beating the game and you'd have a legitimate chance of doing so.**
>
> **But education is different. The challenges you're facing are complex and constantly changing. Therefore, always saying, "Try harder" doesn't guarantee anything—unless you're talking about frustration, burnout, or tanking the morale of your entire team.**

---

* *The bot that beat Tetris in 2021 was developed by Greg Cannon.[22] It took his bot 237 levels to get to the kill screen. But it only took Blue Scuti 157 levels. Therefore, Blue Scuti's accomplishment was more efficient than a computer!*

The Problem is Complex

Society is changing. So are the standards. The needs of students are constantly evolving as well. Therefore, trying to make a difference in education is like trying to hit a target that's perpetually in flux. But not only that. While you're trying to hit this constantly-moving target, chances are good you're also trying to navigate one or more of the following challenges:

> Innovation…
> > Lack of time…
> > > Testing pressures…
> > > > Staffing shortages…
> > > > > Outcome disparities…
> > > > > > A decrease in civility…
> > > > > > > Dwindling resources…
> > > > > > > > A mental health crisis…
> > > > > > > > > Chronic absenteeism…
> > > > > > > > > > Student discipline issues…

These challenges do not exist in a vacuum. They impact the educators who are experiencing them. Moreover, they also impact real, actual students. But there's more. I've heard a number of educators share an additional challenge. This additional challenge is often the result of all the other challenges demanding our attention. So I'm just going to put it out there. *Sometimes it feels like we're being forced to choose who we can help and who needs to wait.* There simply aren't enough resources to address all the needs all the time. I'm not sure if you can relate to the feeling, but I think it might have something to do with a number I'm about to share:

55%

The National Education Association reported a whopping 55% of its members are considering leaving the profession...this is up from 37% in a previous survey.[24] *The number of school administrators who felt the same way was very similar.*[25]

That number should be a call-to-action for policy and decision makers everywhere. My heart hurts for all the educators it represents. Knowing some of the stories behind the number makes it an even harder pill to swallow. But just to be clear, our problem isn't that we have problems—it's the overwhelming complexity of all the problems.

How People Try to Solve Problems

Everyone approaches problems differently. There's not necessarily a right or wrong way to do it. But there are consequences—some beneficial and others not so much.

One approach to overcoming challenges is to just try harder. Blue Scuti's advice seemed to be suggesting this approach. Working harder can be a solid strategy. If you're stuck in a snowstorm—shovel away! But if you are constantly navigating change, you'll need a more sustainable strategy. Which might be why the saying, "Work smarter, not harder" resonates with many educators. Therefore, we're going to explore one way many educators try to work smarter: By drilling down.

In 1989, a team of consultants was hired by the National Parks Service to address a monumental problem—literally. The Lincoln and Jefferson Memorials were deteriorating.[26] The consultants noted that serious structural issues would result if action wasn't taken. Nobody knew it at the time, but the issue they were working on would later be described as "the most famous problem ever solved." Here's why:[26]

In May of 1990, a 50-pound chunk of marble fell from the Jefferson Memorial onto a nearby column. Nobody was injured, but it sent a strong message that something needed to be done. People thought the cleaning chemicals used to treat bird droppings were causing the issue. But that wasn't the case. It was the large volume of water used to clean the droppings that was weakening the structures.

The more water that seeped into the marble and limestone, the more the cracks in the stone would spread. The consultants believed reducing the amount of bird droppings would decrease the amount of water needed to clean the monuments. But they soon discovered bird droppings weren't the problem. The birds were being drawn to the monuments by a large spider population. So they turned their attention to the spiders, eventually learning the spiders were there due to an insect infestation.

Insects known as midges were swarming the monuments at night. People had assumed all the droppings* were from birds. However, the majority of the droppings were actually from the midges. The insects were being attracted by the flood lights used to light up the monuments at sunset.

Armed with this information, they delayed turning the lights on by thirty minutes each evening and saw an 85% reduction in the number of insects.[26] The monument story is attributed to a research report by Donald Messersmith. Leaders have used the story to demonstrate the importance of drilling down to find the root cause of issues.

As educators, we have had a lot of practice trying to get to the bottom of issues. We form Student Support Teams, Instructional Leadership Teams, and a bunch of other committees that meet a lot. I'd say we do a fair amount of drilling down on our own too.

---

*Female midges usually drop their egg masses over water. The eggs sink to the bottom and hatch within a week's time. When dropped on stone, the eggs form a dark mass that is not easy to clean up.[27] And evidently, the masses look a lot like bird doo doo.

> If time wasn't an issue, we could conduct a root-cause analysis for every complex challenge that comes our way. But time is an issue. Pretending it's not, is a recipe for frustration.

Priority-Selection (Exercise)

There's another approach to overcoming challenges that's quite common. It goes by a few different names, including: putting out fires, addressing immediate concerns, and managing chaos. But I'm going to refer to it as *choosing the priority*. Anytime you elevate the importance of one thing over another, you're *choosing the priority*.

If you've ever seen a kindergarten teacher stop in the middle of a lesson to tell a student who is crossing his legs and doing the "potty dance" to use the restroom, you know what *choosing the priority* looks like. However, *choosing the priority* isn't just something you do in the heat of the moment.

OVERCOMING EDUCATION EXERCISE
PRIORITY-SELECTION SCENARIO

For this exercise, imagine you're choosing the priorities you'll focus on for the upcoming year. I recognize that we often spend months poring over data to make decisions like the one you're about to make. However, this exercise was designed to take ten minutes or less. The bulk of that time should go to step four. So try not to overthink the first few steps. The first three steps should feel fast and that's by design.

SKILLS AND COMPETENCIES

WHAT ARE YOUR TOP PRIORITIES AS A LEADER?

DATA (DATA USE AND PRIVACY)	CULTURAL COMPETENCE	TECHNOLOGY	PARTNERSHIP AND BRIDGE BUILDER
RESOURCE ALLOCATION	VISION AND CATALYST FOR CHANGE	SUPPORT AND SUPERVISION	PROFESSIONAL LEARNING
HUMAN RESOURCE MANAGEMENT	POLICY AND LAW	STUDENT NEEDS (INCL. HEALTH, SAFETY, AND WELL BEING)	PERSONALIZED LEARNING
PEOPLE SKILLS	CURRICULUM, INSTRUCTION, ASSESSMENT	RELATIONSHIPS AND CONNECTION	INNOVATION
COLLABORATION AND COLLECTIVE GENIUS	LEARNING STRATEGIES AND PEDAGOGY	CONTINUOUS IMPROVEMENT	DECISION MAKING
FOSTERING TRUST	CLIMATE AND CULTURE	INTEGRITY	TECHNICAL AND ADAPTIVE CHANGE
PERSONAL AND PROFESSIONAL HARMONY	CRISIS MANAGEMENT	INSTRUCTIONALLY CENTERED CONVERSATIONS	?

(FUTURE READY SCHOOLS, 2023; GRISSOM ET AL., 2021; GUSTAFSON, 2015; HILL ET AL., 2022; LAMBERT & BOUCHAMMA, 2019)

Figure 1.1: Skills and competencies grid

Directions for Priority-Selection Exercise:

1. Start by skimming the skills and competencies in the grid (see figure 1.1).
2. Next, if you notice something important is missing, write it in the space with the question mark.
3. Then, select one priority to focus on. Place a star by it.

4. Finally, think about the priority you selected in the previous step. I'm going to invite you to deconstruct your priority by brainstorming the sub-skills or things needed to make your priority possible. Another way to think about this is in terms of a recipe. Try to list the ingredients needed to make the priority you selected successful.

The point of the priority-selection exercise isn't to generate an exhaustive list of sub-skills. It's to pause and consider why *choosing the priority* isn't always as easy or straightforward as it might sound. Priorities are complex. People don't always view them the same way. Even if everyone on your team selected the same priority, it's possible your ingredient lists would look different.

Deconstructing Innovation

I asked open AI to deconstruct "Innovation" just for fun. The sub-skills I got back included adaptability, creativity, and risk management, among other things. I created a visual representation of the sub-skills needed to make innovation possible (see figure 1.2).

Now, imagine how "Innovation" would change depending on who is thinking about the ingredients. For example, if somebody–like your school district's legal counsel–were to look at innovation through an intense focus on "risk management," there's a chance it could mitigate the benefits of creativity, adaptability, and innovation altogether.

Case in point: I once walked on stage at a state conference to deliver a keynote called, "The Future is Now." Just moments before speaking, a leader asked me to avoid talking about drones. The rest of what he said was a blur. Because the message I had planned to share did reference drones–as part of a sequence on innovative instructional leadership. Everything worked out–and I didn't crash any of the drones I flew

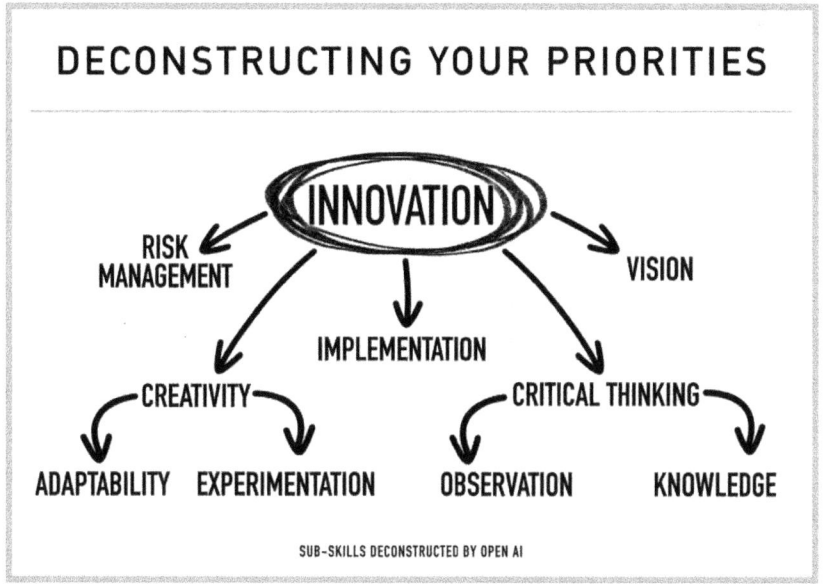

Figure 1.2: Deconstructing innovation

during the keynote (just kidding!). But the story demonstrates how people can look at the same priority and see different things. Priorities can be complex.

Another thing that makes *choosing the priority* a challenge is volume. And I'm not talking about how loud your lunchroom is either. The number of decisions educators make is intense. I've read that teachers make more than 1,500 decisions in a day–a number comparable to air-traffic controllers.[28] And I'd bet a good portion of these decisions involve *choosing the priority*.

> Like all strategies, *choosing the priority* can be helpful. But choosing priorities alone doesn't solve complex problems. If it did, more than half of all educators would not be contemplating a career change.

What About Relationships?!

If you and I had completed the priority-selection exercise together, I would've asked you what you picked. So if you or somebody on your team thinks of it, I'd love for you to share your priorities and how you deconstructed them. Feel free to tag me on social media or add #OvercomingEducation so I can see what you came up with.

However, if I had to guess one priority that you might have selected, I'd lean towards building relationships. Because people talk about relationships a lot. I'd estimate 93% of people that I interview mention relationships* as being a top priority. You might see this as a positive. However, very few educators are able to explain the steps they take to build relationships—or why they take these steps.

People are not as fluent in talking about their practice in this area as you might think. It could be that building relationships just comes instinctively to many people. Or maybe I just need to get better at asking interview questions. Either way, relationships involve nuanced thinking and skills within skills.

Instead of saying, "It's all about relationships," maybe we should start saying, "It's all about empathy, trust, listening, integrity, communication, teamwork, and mutual respect." And then commit to creating the conditions where these things are core components of the culture.

It's not outside the realm of possibility that you are working with a parent, co-worker, or supervisor who believes wholeheartedly that relationships are a priority. Yet, when you interact with that person, the last thing you might feel is more connected to them. This is because simply *choosing the priority* doesn't mean others will experience it in a positive or productive manner. Even if everyone agrees it's a priority!

---

* *In all the interview responses I've ever heard, communication is the only other thing that rivals the frequency in which relationships have been brought up. Regardless of the position we're hiring for, applicants mention these two things more than any other.*

Hopefully, you're starting to see why just "working harder" or constantly trying to *choose the priority* can't be our only strategies. If not, here's some social proof that might help.

The Jam Stand Experiment

In the priority-selection exercise, you had 27+ priorities to choose from. I provided a large number of options because they all seemed important. But there was another reason. I wanted you to experience why *choosing the priority* doesn't always work.

In 2000, psychologists from Columbia and Stanford University set up a series of experiments.[29] They were curious about the popular belief that having more choices is better. So they set up a jam stand inside a grocery store. The jam stand was open for two weekends. And researchers rotated between offering six flavors and thirty flavors every hour. They wanted to see how shoppers interacted with the limited-choice stand compared to the extensive-choice stand.

Predictably, the stand with thirty jam flavors attracted more shoppers. Of the 754 people who visited the grocery store, 60% stopped at the stand with thirty flavors of jam. Yet, there was a striking difference when it came to making a purchase.

Ten times more people bought jam from the stand with fewer options (see figure 1.3). To put this in business terms, the stand with only six choices saw a 30% conversion rate when it came to turning potential customers into buyers. The stand with thirty choices had a meager conversion rate of 3%. Not only that, but customers experienced a higher satisfaction rate at the stand with fewer options. (Fewer options meant less buyer's remorse!)

When people have too many choices, they tend to respond in one of four ways:[28]

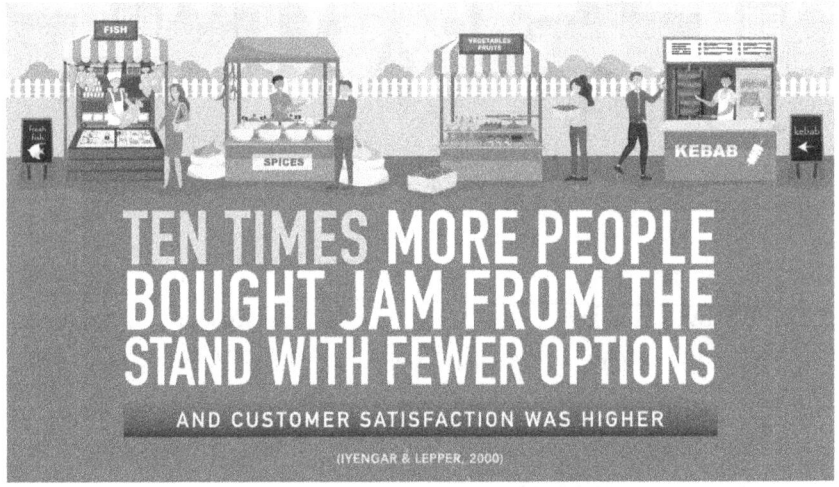

Figure 1.3: The jam stand experiment

1. They defer the decision.
2. They search for additional options.
3. They choose the default option.
4. They simply opt not to choose.

As eccentric as the jam stand experiment might sound, there are some parallels to how *choosing the priority* plays out in schools. Maybe you responded to the priority-selection exercise in one of the four ways above as well?!

> Trying to choose from *all the things* gets in the way of choosing the *most important things*. Sometimes it even makes us choose *none of the things*.

Another Win

We paused to celebrate YOU in the introduction of this book. And we're going to do it again. Because now you have a better understanding of some of the common approaches people use to overcome challenges. But you also know a few reasons why these approaches don't always work out so well. Which is a big deal!

Just to be clear, I'm not suggesting any of these approaches are bad. There is nothing wrong with trying harder, drilling down to root causes, or choosing the priorities that matter most. In fact, I'd encourage you to continue doing these things when it makes sense to do so.

There is another reason I think we should celebrate. You've reached a turning point in this book. We've covered a lot of ground. But from this point on, we're going to start going deeper into how and why the fluencies work. So that you and your team can live out the core message of this book. Here it is again:

> **Complex challenges can be overwhelming.
> But making a difference doesn't have to be.**

Reduction is Essential

The framework in this book was informed by research, leadership experience, and my work with schools and organizations across the country. However, it took me reading a story from the technology sector to finally be able to distill things down into the essence of making a difference.

Steve Jobs was more than an entrepreneur and CEO. He was a visionary leader who helped conceive some of Apple's greatest products. But most people are less familiar with the creative genius at Apple who helped Jobs "think different." Jony Ive joined Apple in September of 1992.[30] Many of the products you and I use today have been influenced by Jony Ive's commitment to simplicity. The iPhone is a perfect example of this. Yet, the iPhone would not exist had it not been for a moment of radical focus from Steve Jobs.

OVERCOMING EDUCATION

When Steve Jobs returned to Apple in 1997, the company had more than forty products on the market. Jobs struggled to make sense of the massive portfolio. But he wasn't alone. Apple had so many products, its employees had a hard time understanding them all.

There's a story in which Jobs stopped a meeting, erased a whiteboard, and drew a simple two-by-two grid.[30] Next, he wrote the words "Consumer" and "Professional" across the top, and "Portable" and "Desktop" on the side. These four words became the foundation of Apple's product strategy moving forward.

Jony Ive helped implement the strategy with dramatic results. I'm not sure where Apple would be right now if Steve Jobs and Jony Ive would have tried leading from a larger grid. But I do know what it feels like to try and juggle too many priorities at a time.

We know education is not the same as Apple or the technology sector. But some of the same science that helped Apple's design, manufacturing, and marketing teams achieve unimaginable success can be leveraged to help us overcome complexity. Because our brains are designed to see patterns.[31]

The outermost layer of the brain—known as the neocortex—has a powerful ability. Within all the wrinkles and folds of the neocortex* are 300 million neurons specially designed to find familiar things. Your brain's uncanny ability to quickly pull out patterns hidden in complex challenges is what makes the framework for this book work.

There are a lot of priorities in education, which is why it can be so exhausting to constantly choose. But your brain is a pattern-seeking machine. So let's teach it to find a pattern that can actually help you and your team overcome challenges.

---

* *Only mammals have the neocortex. And it accounts for approximately 80% of the weight of your brain.*[31]

> **Let's reduce your focus to increase your impact.**

The 5-Fluency Framework

There are many ways to learn. There are many different ways to lead and make a difference, too. People have been using variations of individual fluencies in and out of education for years. Core competencies is not a new concept. But focusing on the five essential fluencies within the framework is different—and it can help you and your team make a difference across multiple environments (see figure 1.4).

As a friendly reminder, I'm not saying the fluencies and framework are the only way. In fact, I designed the framework so it would connect to the work and priorities you and your team have already established. Therefore, the framework is intended to elevate your work and thinking—not supplant it.

There is a good chance you're already using the fluencies. Like when you're building relationships, trust, and integrity. And when you're leading continuous improvement efforts, change, and co-creating systems to better support all students. The fluencies represent the essence of adaptive work. They are open-ended by design.

Each chapter of this book is focused on helping you hone and develop your skills with one of the fluencies. Within each chapter, I will also help you connect and combine fluencies to maximize the difference you can make. Here's a brief overview of each fluency in the framework:

Who You Want to Be

The dot in the middle of the matrix represents the essence of *Who you want to be* as an educator. Whether you realize it or not, that dot can change everything. So much so, I consider it a super-fluency. Learning to access *Who you want to be* will help you leverage the other fluencies with purpose and intention.

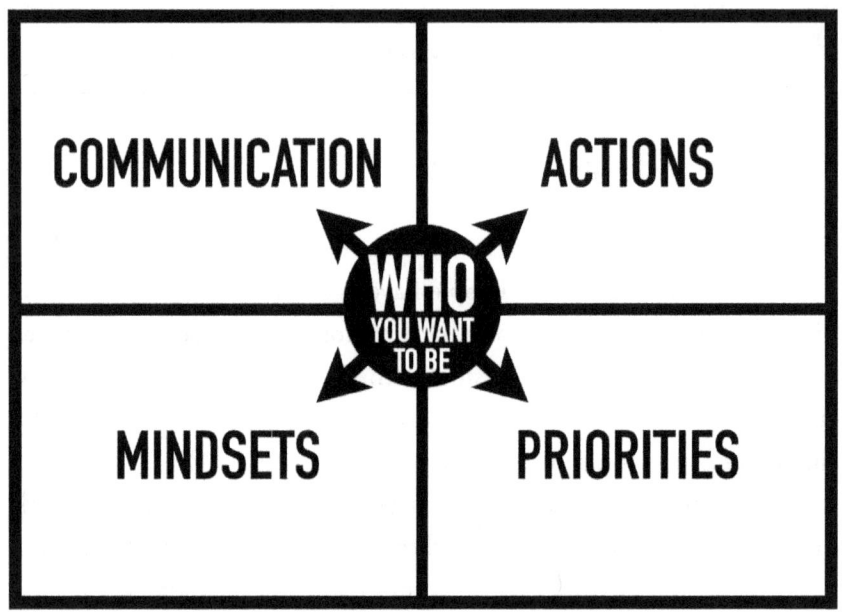

Figure 1.4: The 5-Fluency Framework

Mindsets
Mindsets refer to more than your beliefs or mood on a given day. They are the stories you quietly tell yourself. They influence your posture towards challenges and how you view the opportunities in front of you. Your mindsets are a force to be reckoned with. So you want them on your side.

Communication
We engage in conversations, exchange emails, and attend meetings not everyone wants to be at. But these things are often an illusion that communication has taken place. Communication is like the oil in a powerful engine. Without clear and consistent communication, the efforts and potential of your team will sputter.

Priorities
Priorities are the drivers of our words and actions. Everyone has them. Learning how to co-create and carry priorities with your team will make the work more meaningful and manageable.

Actions
Actions are the receipts for the priorities you hold and promises you make. Sometimes educators need to make difficult decisions. In these moments, you want to ensure your actions reflect *Who you want to be*.

The 5-Fluency Framework is based on elements of practice that have proven to be effective time and time again. Whether you're trying to create a more student-centered learning environment, develop a culture of literacy, or partnering with a person who is not easy to work with. The fluencies can help.

The Best Movies Ever Made

Reading this book can help you make a difference—without having to change careers or implode your aspirations of having a life outside school. You can make a difference through small and intentional investments of time and energy.

Yet, I want to be extremely clear about something before I share a story involving the entertainment industry. (This is mainly for anyone reading who is not working in education.) **Schools should be fully funded and supported as the critical priority they are. Educators should not have to work multiple jobs to make a living. This story is about the power we have when we make small and intentional investments of time—not the further gutting of school budgets.**

One of my all-time favorite movies is *Star Wars*. Just don't ask me which one. I love them all. For me, a big part of what makes a movie great is who I'm watching it with. The candy selection factors heavily into the equation as well. However, Hollywood has a more official formula for determining box-office hits. They rely on opening release data, domestic sales, and international numbers.[32] All this data goes into which movies are immortalized as all-time greats (see figure 1.5).

ALL-TIME WORLDWIDE TOP GROSSING MOVIES
BOX OFFICE BILLIONS

RANK	MOVIE (YEAR)	$
1.	AVATAR (2009)	$2.9
2.	AVENGERS: ENDGAME (2019)	$2.8
3.	AVATAR: THE WAY OF WATER (2022)	$2.3
4.	TITANIC (1997)	$2.3
5.	STAR WARS: THE FORCE AWAKENS (2015)	$2.1
6.	AVENGERS: INFINITY WAR (2018)	$2.1
7.	SPIDER-MAN: NO WAY HOME (2021)	$1.9
8.	JURASSIC WORLD (2015)	$1.7
9.	THE LION KING (2019)	$1.7
10.	THE AVENGERS (2012)	$1.5

BOXOFFICEMOJO.COM (DEC. 2023)   OVERCOMING EDUCATION (B. GUSTAFSON)

Figure 1.5: All-time best movies

I recently crunched some numbers to see how much the all-time best movies made altogether compared to the size of their combined budgets. I got the idea to look at box-office numbers this way from a website called *Information is Beautiful*.[33] You might be surprised at what I found:

20.3 BILLION

The total worldwide sales of the top-grossing movies is a jaw-dropping $20,300,000,000.

2.5 BILLION

The budgets from all ten of the top-grossing movies was around $2,526,000,000. These costs cover production, paychecks, marketing, and more.

704%

Here's where this gets really interesting. The percentage of the overall budget the top-grossing movies recovered was a whopping 704%! Based on this calculation, the business of making blockbuster movies appears to be booming.*

But this is not the end of the story. There's another number you need to see. It reminds us that small and solvable things can make an enormous difference.

In 2002, a movie starring Nia Vardalos and John Corbett was released. The movie had a modest budget of $5 million dollars. Although it never made the number one spot at the box office, it made $368 million, making it one of the highest grossing independent films of all time.[34, 35]

The movie was called, *My Big Fat Greek Wedding*. But what I really want you to see is the percentage of the budget the movie recovered:[35]

7,375%

That's the number! It is exponentially higher than every movie on the all-time best list. All of those high-budget films recovered

---

* The percentage of the budget a movie earns back focuses on the recovery of the production budget. The return on investment (ROI) looks at overall profitability in terms of revenue streams and expenses. Both measures help us understand a movie's financial performance, but they are not the same.

704%—which isn't exactly chump change. But this modest film recovered significantly more. Think about that!

This story is a form of social proof that suggests you may not have to sacrifice your friends, family, and sanity in order to make a difference in education. Small and strategic investments of time, energy, and focus can make an exponentially positive difference.

One More Thing We Need to Invest In

If everything is a priority, nothing is the priority. Ultimately, you and your team need to decide what to prioritize and where to invest your time and attention. But this won't stop me from making a few suggestions as you make these decisions.

I read some fascinating research about the connection between emotional intelligence and educator well-being.[36] The study had a large and representative sample involving educators from 48 states and part of Canada.

Participants in the study were asked to identify the three feelings they experienced most when working in their school,[36] using one-word responses. The Venn Diagram shows some of the most frequent responses (see figure 1.6).

Before we explore the diagram together, I want to invite you to take a little time to study it. What do you notice? What do you wonder?

I can see from the center of the diagram that both groups of educators experienced a range of emotions. From *busy* and *anxious* to being *energized, hopeful,* and *proud.* However, I also see that each group had some distinctly different feelings. Like being *disrespected, angry,* and *unsupported* on one side. But being *motivated, grateful,* and *enthusiastic* on the other.

It would be easy to try and connect these feelings to educator effectiveness or educator outcomes. But what if I told you this study wasn't

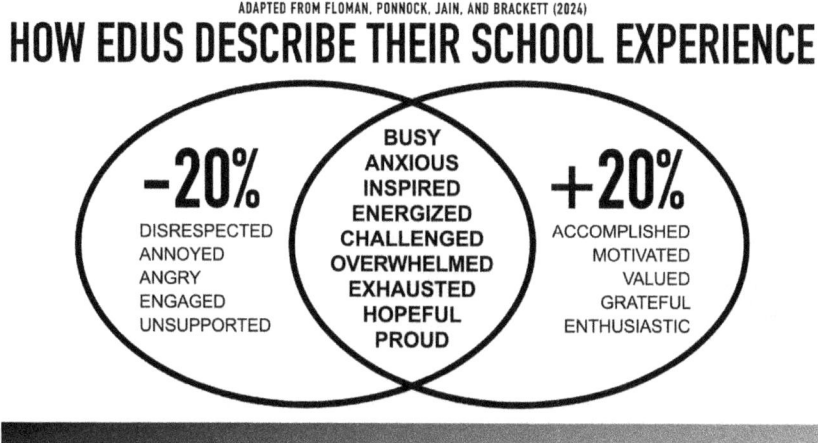

Figure 1.6: How educators describe their school experience

about teachers at all? It was about leadership. Let's drill down a little further.

When educators perceive their leaders as having higher emotional regulation and support, they feel better about their experience at school. A lot better. But when leaders are perceived as having lower emotional regulation and support, their teams feel worse about work. Here's an updated diagram showing the context that was missing initially (see figure 1.7). The researchers linked these findings to emotional contagion theory–feelings spread.[37]

Even though this study focused on the impact principals have on staff well-being, we know there are many leaders in a school, both formal and informal. Adults and students. Therefore, it's possible people will pick-up on the emotional cues of *anyone* perceived as having influence–regardless of positional authority.

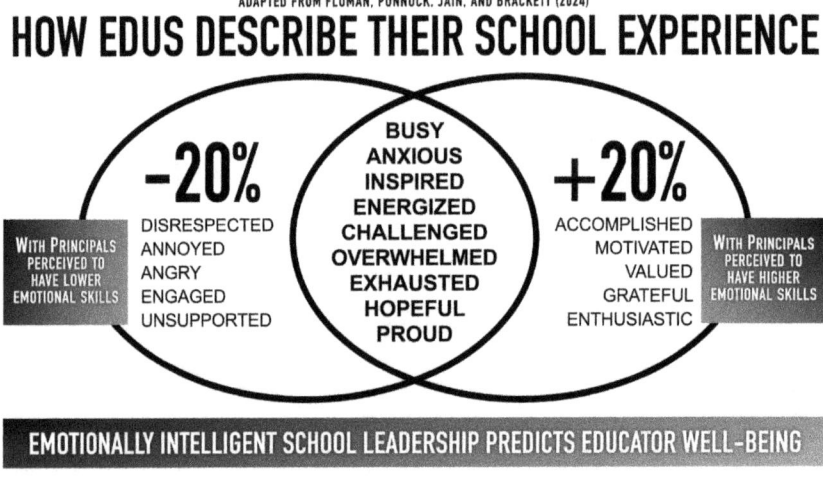

Figure 1.7: Emotionally intelligent leaders impact others

> I share this with you because how you want your leadership to look, sound, and feel matters. As you and your team learn how to use the framework and fluencies to make a difference, be intentional with where you focus your energy. Focus is contagious.

Validating Doubt and Disbelief

I want the books I read to be practical—unless I'm reading an epic sci-fi adventure. Then, I need it to have complex characters, epic world-building, and a ridiculously suspenseful ticking time bomb. But this book isn't sci-fi. Therefore, I'm going to remove all the suspense.

This book contains a combination of storytelling, psychology, and research from several different sectors—including education. But it also contains checkpoints like this. I'm hoping that addressing some of your questions and hesitations in this manner makes our journey practical and fun. If a particular doubt or objection doesn't apply to you, feel free to skip ahead to the next section.

You might be wondering:
*"How are Hollywood movies, a teenage Tetris prodigy,
and the psychology of jam sales relevant to my role in education…"*

This is a fair question. (And I'm smiling right now because there are a couple of aspects I want to address here.) I believe education transcends the work we do in schools. Our profession empowers every other profession. Therefore, there's a strong connection between the work we get to do every day and the breakthroughs occurring in other sectors. We can learn a lot from each other.

However, there's another aspect to the stories and research I'll be sharing. This book is for educators who are providing leadership at every level of the profession—not just those serving in formal leadership positions. It is about learning how to persevere, make a difference, and work with people who are not the same as you. So my decision to use examples from education and beyond was purposeful.

Lastly, our profession is filled with people who possess diverse talents and backgrounds. The stories I've selected are designed to inspire you to *think* and *feel*—even if you're reading about another person's passions and journey.

Or you might be wondering…
*"I'm noticing quite a few connections to psychology…
are you trying to portray yourself as a psychologist?!"*

Goodness, no! I am NOT a psychologist. I'm a practicing principal. But many of the stories and strategies in this book are connected to research on human behavior and thinking. Providing you with more than just my opinions and personal experiences was important to me. Of course, I'll share some opinions as well.

The Heart of the Matter

The National Parks Service solved a monumental problem–by drilling down. And the solution made sense. But not to everyone.

Photographers pushed back hard on the idea. Adjusting the hours the floodlights were on impacted the quality of their photographs. Their pushback eventually prompted the National Parks Service to turn the lights back on and they began exploring other solutions like netting, spikes, and plastic barriers.[26]

Complex challenges can be hard for a lot of different reasons. They are dynamic, multi-faceted, and can be emotional at times too. Which brings us to the heart of the matter–and the heart of this book.

I promise this book will help you and your team learn to see the small and solvable parts hidden inside every complex challenge. I can't promise everyone will agree with your approach all the time. (They won't.) I can't promise your challenges will go away overnight either. But I know the chances of you making a difference will go up dramatically as you learn how to access and apply five essential fluencies:

Who you want to be can positively influence everything you do moving forward. It is truly a super-fluency.

Mindsets are more than having positivity and a growth-oriented outlook. They involve developing mental structures to help you approach challenges with agility.

Communication starts from within. The language of connection flows from authenticity and trust.

Priorities are hard to carry alone. Meeting people where they're at will help you co-create priorities you can carry together.

Actions transform your ideals into tangible experiences. I'll help you get started by sharing some subtle shifts you can make right away.

You don't have to overextend yourself to make a difference. This is a message I'll be reminding you of often. Not because I think you'll forget. But because we live in a culture that bombards us with a different message. Yet, the story of Steve Jobs, Jony Ive, and a grocery store jam stand experiment serve as social proof that "more" doesn't mean better.

There is power in reduction. I'm going to help you practice it. Starting with a simple decision that could elevate everything you'll ever do. We'll get to that decision in Chapter 2. But first, here's that message we want to feel like second nature:

> **Complex challenges can be overwhelming.
> But making a difference doesn't have to be. Overcoming is a skill. Therefore, you can practice it.**

CHAPTER 2

The Power of "Who You Want to Be"

You are already winning! You understand why people show up to challenges predisposed to just try harder. Or search for bigger solutions. But you also know that narrowing your focus and practicing reduction can be more effective—and you have some stories, statistics, and box-office receipts to back it up. In this chapter, we'll keep the victory train rolling using a series of interactive exercises, including:

1.) We'll explore the psychology behind why naming challenges is critical to making progress. And we'll practice it too. (THAT'S A WIN!)
2.) I'll also show you how to apply the 5-Fluency Framework to your challenges. (HUGE WIN!)

If that's not enough, I'll help you craft a leadership* statement you can actually use. (BONUS!)

The Banyan Tree

Sometimes you don't recognize the value of something until it's gone. Other times, you know a thing is valuable, so you hold on tight and count your blessings. This is a chapter about moving from the former to the latter.

People had no idea what was about to unfold in the historic town of Lahaina on August 8, 2023.[38] That is the date the worst natural disaster in the history of Hawaii was unleashed.

At approximately 6:40 a.m., high winds forced powerlines to the ground which sparked several small wildfires. A short time later, officials thought they had the brush fires 100% contained. But by 3:30 p.m., it was clear this wasn't the case. As flames ripped through the historic downtown, they disintegrated everything in their path.

Many people fled to the ocean for protection from the intense heat. However, it's estimated that one hundred people perished in the blaze. But the devastation didn't stop there. Arsenic, dust, and lead from the paint in Luhaina's historic houses turned the town into a toxic parking lot. It was uninhabitable for months. People were eventually allowed back to their homes but had to wear hazmat suits. Finding closure in the ashes proved very difficult.[39]

Heat from the wildfires had been so extreme, some said it altered the soil's ability to absorb water.[40] Therefore, the trees, fauna, and hope itself seemed to be endangered. The people of Luhaina did not need a reminder of the devastation. Yet, standing in the courthouse square on

---

* Remember: I use the terms "leader" and "educator" interchangeably. There's no doubt in my mind that you and your team show leadership every day. Many educators are leaning into challenges that are more complex than those faced by people serving in formal leadership roles outside education.

Luhaina's famous Front Street stood a severely burned Banyan Tree. The fabled tree had been part of the town's heart and history for 150 years. It seemed the tree and all it represented were history now, too.

But a month after the fire, the Banyan Tree started showing signs of life.[41] New growth was discovered on the charred remains. Its core was alive.

With the signs of regeneration came a massive effort to help the tree fight its way back. Volunteers and contractors started treating the soil, attempting to help water penetrate the earth again. It was not an easy task, but they eventually found a way to get water to the tree's root system. The Banyan Tree is a symbol of hope. But not just for citizens of Luhaina. The tree is a testament to the power you have inside.

Educators are facing some incredible challenges. It's easy to lose sight of this power when things around you constantly compete for your attention. But the power is there. Which means it's possible to draw from it.

> **You have the potential to breathe new life into challenging situations. But you must decide "*Who you want to be*" first.**

Comparing with Intention

My wife and I often reference a quote when chatting with our three kids: "Comparing leads to discontentment." When one of our kids is struggling, it is often connected to a comparison they're making. Sometimes the comparison is obvious. Like when they want something a friend or another family has. Other times it might be more abstract. Like when they slip into comparing themselves to who the world is telling them they should be. The cautionary message we've given our kids about comparing has been pretty consistent. But I recently learned about an exception to the rule.

There is one situation in which comparison can be a positive thing. Researchers found comparing who you actually are to *Who you want to be* is helpful.[42] To be clear, this comparison isn't about trying to be somebody else. It's about trying to be the best version of you.

In psychology, the term "self-discrepancy" refers to the gap between how you see yourself and who you aspire to be.[42] It's like comparing who you are right now to the ideal version of you. It sounds easy enough. But people don't always do this intuitively.

We're more prone to compare ourselves to another person or job description. A meta-analysis of seventy studies found comparing your actual self to your job description doesn't have much impact.[42] But comparing your actual self to *Who you want to be* does.

Over the course of this chapter, I'm going to help you reflect on *Who you want to be* as an educator. But I'm also going to provide you tools to move closer to being that ideal version of yourself so that you and your team can access your ideal selves—especially when you're facing complex challenges.

"Who Do You Want to Be?" on the Continuum (Exercise)

Despite the long title this is one of the shortest exercises in the entire book. Completing it will make the numbers I share immediately following the exercise more interesting (and fun).

OVERCOMING EDUCATION EXERCISE
"WHO YOU WANT TO BE" ON THE CONTINUUM

THE POWER OF "WHO YOU WANT TO BE"

Take a second to place yourself on this continuum (see figure 2.1). Feel free to place an "X" where you think you are—or just make a mental note.

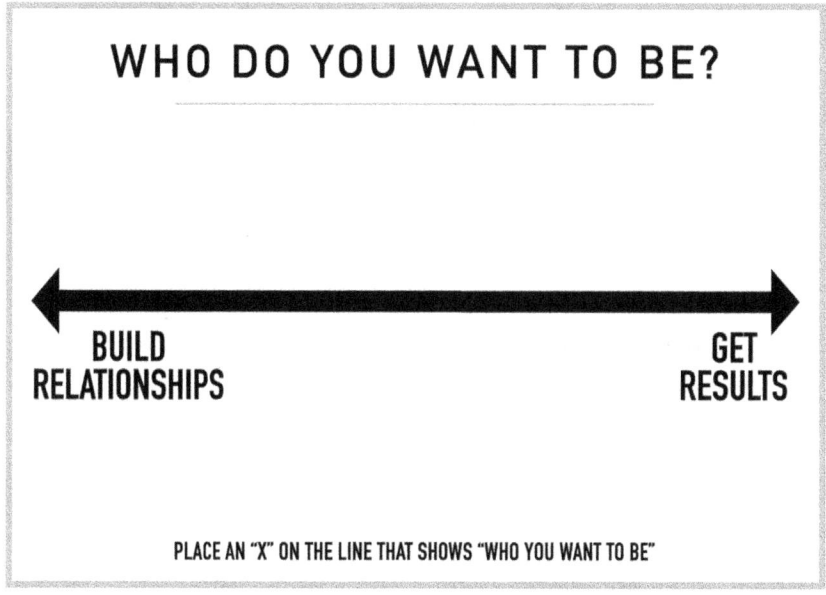

Figure 2.1: Relationships-results continuum

Now, I want to invite you to think about where other people perceive you to be on the continuum. Would they say you're more focused on relationships or results? Once you have an idea in your mind, you'll want to see a few numbers:

12 - 14%

In one study, leaders who were perceived as "strong" in social skills—like communication, empathy, and building relationships—only had a 12% chance of being viewed as great leaders.[43] *Those who were perceived as "strong" in their ability to get results only had a 14% chance of being viewed as great leaders.*

72%

However, leaders who were perceived as "strong" in both their focus on relationships and results had a 72% chance of being viewed as great leaders.[43] Which is significantly more than the 12-14% chance those who were perceived as leading for one or the other had.

Knowing these numbers makes the choice seem obvious. Being a leader who cares about both—relationships and results—is important. But here's the thing. A separate study that spanned ten years and involved 60,000 participants from four different continents shows things are not as obvious (or easy) as they might seem.[44]

<1%

Researchers found less than 1% of bosses were rated high in both a results focus and relationships focus. LESS than 1%!

We might think the choice to focus on both should be obvious. But this doesn't mean it's easy to do. There was a period in my career when this continuum wasn't something I gave much thought to. Looking back, I was probably focused on a combination of trying to support others and trying to focus on my to-do list. I suppose this could've been a form of me trying to care about both. However, I know I wasn't bringing intention to *Who I wanted to be*.

To be clear, deciding *Who you want to be* involves more than choosing between relationships and results. It is a journey involving aspirational thinking, reflecting upon your authentic self, and the context you're working in. But rest assured, every second you invest into this super-fluency will pay dividends in the long run.

Crafting *"Who You Want to Be"* (Exercise)

As leaders, we want to make a positive difference. Deciding *Who you want to be*, and bringing that ideal version of yourself to challenges is one way to do it.

I've already mentioned how I use the terms "educator" and "leader" interchangeably. This isn't to remove the responsibility that those of us serving in formal leadership roles must do better. Instead, it's to acknowledge and empower everyone who is actually leading–regardless of position or title.

With that said, we're going to explore the essence of *Who you want to be*. Before we do, think about the story of the charred Banyan tree. Unbeknownst to many people who visited the island, the core of that tree held limitless potential. Just like you do! **When you decide *Who you want to be*, you decide what parts of you will grow and what parts need to go.**

OVERCOMING EDUCATION EXERCISE
CRAFTING "WHO YOU WANT TO BE"

The steps below build upon each other. You can complete them individually or with your team. To complete them together simply switch out the word "you" with "we," "us," or "our team." It's OK to respond to the prompts with your first-draft thinking. Your thinking will likely evolve as you progress through the book. *Note: I adapted this exercise from a book I read (and loved) by A.J. Harper.*[45]

1. First, write down a few words that describe *Who you want to be* as an educator. You're on the right track if whatever you write inspires and challenges you. I aspire to be a leader who:

   _____
   _____.

2. Next, think about your purpose. Try to describe what it looks like when your purpose is fulfilled. My purpose is:

   _____
   _____
   _____.

3. Then, write down the reason your purpose matters to you. Because:

   _____
   _____.

4. Finally, take what you've written in the first three steps and complete the statement below. I aspire to be a leader who:

   _____
   _____.

   My purpose is _____.
   because _____.

I obviously don't know what you wrote (or *if* you wrote). However, I am willing to bet you want to make a difference in some way. When we get to the core of *Who we want to be*, we often find a desire to elevate others, advocate, help, transform, serve, inspire, or some combination of these goals. You might want something different as well.

I can relate. One of the more nuanced parts of *Who I want to be* involves bringing a sense of calm to chaotic situations so that others can access their best thinking. This is not a grandiose goal. But I know when I'm able to walk in my purpose it makes a difference.

Deciding *Who you want to be* is more than a theoretical construct. Making the difference you aspire to make requires you to take steps towards actually being that person. Which isn't always easy.

Isabella Baumfree

There will be people in your life and leadership journey who try to tell you who you're not. Just remember–they don't get to decide *Who you want to be*. I'm not aware of a more courageous example of this than the one set by Isabella Baumfree.[46]

Baumfree knew *Who she wanted to be*. She also understood the inherent worth she already had, despite facing extreme suffering and oppression. Baumfree was enslaved at birth. By the time she was thirty years old, she had been bought and sold four times and had five children. She was no stranger to physical abuse and forced labor. But there's a lot more to her story.[46, 47]

In 1827, she escaped with one of her babies, Sofia. A year later, Baumfree sued a white man in an effort to have her son, Peter, returned. It was the first time in history a Black woman won such a case.[46]

Baumfree went on to become a charismatic speaker, itinerant preacher, and championed women's rights and the abolition of slavery. In 1843, she shared that the Holy Spirit had called her to speak the truth. Which is why you may know her by another name: Sojourner Truth. Despite never being taught to read or write, Truth dictated an autobiography that has impacted countless people. She was able to make a living from the proceeds of her book while continuing her work as a lecturer and activist.

Truth connected with William Lloyd Garrison and Fredrick Douglas through this work. While her mission aligned with what they were doing, she eventually separated herself from Douglas, who believed formerly enslaved men should be given voting rights before women.

If you want to know who Sojourner Truth was, study the essence of her actions. They offer a glimpse into her heart, soul, and *Who she wanted to be*.

We all face challenges. But some people face them with a stronger sense of purpose than others. This doesn't happen by accident.

> Deciding *Who you want to be* is not the hard part.
> But being that person when things are not going your way will challenge you to your core. Yet, if there's one challenge worth overcoming in your life–this might be it.

Name Your Challenges (Exercise)

Acknowledging the things that make the work we get to do challenging is an important step in overcoming them. It's also supported by neuroscience.[48] Naming your challenges helps you move from the automatic response regions of the brain to the regions that help you access your best thinking.

In one study, negative images were shown to people as their brains were being monitored.[48] Researchers asked people to name the images and emotions they were feeling as each image was displayed. As they named these things, their neural activity shifted from the amygdala to the prefrontal cortex.

The amygdala is the region in your brain responsible for emotional processing, fear, and threat responses–like fight, flight, or freeze.[49] However, your prefrontal cortex does just the opposite. It helps you regulate your emotions so you can access your best thinking. Therefore, naming your challenges and feelings moves you from the fight, flight, or freeze region in your brain to the part of your brain that can help you access and apply *Who you want to be*.

OVERCOMING EDUCATION EXERCISE
NAME YOUR CHALLENGES

Naming challenges can be something you do alone or with your team. I'm going to invite you to list the top eight things you struggle with in education. There's nothing magic about the number eight—except when I lead workshops on overcoming barriers, I often invite participants to engage in a challenge where they try to generate their top eight struggles on a giant game board.

It is OK to list challenges your team or co-workers are struggling with too. However, do not write the names of specific people on any of the lines. The point of this activity is to acknowledge what's difficult so your brain can respond to that reality from an effective place. It is not to levy blame against a specific person or department.

It's also OK if you're not ready to share your challenges. I trust whatever you decide is right for you. Consider this exercise an opportunity to practice being *Who you want to be*.

1. Name some of the challenges you or your team are experiencing.
   _____
   _____
   _____
   _____
   _____

In my work as a principal, I've used a similar exercise with individuals and teams who are feeling overwhelmed or needing support. It can feel energizing to name what's hard. But we usually don't stop there. We also pick out a few of the challenges on our list that feel the most pressing. Then, we'll choose one to focus on right away—being sure to select a challenge that includes elements that are within our control.

Naming, Blaming, and Reframing

Research using brain imaging from Duke University found people process positive events with their prefrontal cortex. However, negative events are processed by the amygdala.[50] Therefore, it's not as easy to experience negative events and then seamlessly shift to naming them in a productive manner. Your brain will resist this due to the regions involved, so it will take some intention.

Even when you are able to practice naming—and activating your prefrontal cortex—you'll want to be on the lookout. There's a mind trap that will take you to an unproductive place faster than you can say, "The internet is down again?!" That mind trap is *blame*.

Blame activates your amygdala—that region of the brain involved with your body's fight, flight, or freeze response.[50] Which means all the progress you made moving to the prefrontal cortex is undone when you slip into "blaming" mode. Because blame brings you right back to the amygdala.

Blame can take many forms, so don't think you're in the clear just yet. First, blame is more than blatantly throwing somebody under the bus. It can be subtle and insidious. Phrases like "they decided" or "the district" can disassociate us from a challenge. I'm not judging anyone who uses these terms. I'm not telling you that you need to take the fall for somebody else's mistakes either. But I am saying this is a slippery slope with a very real impact on your brain.

However, it's not just your brain that can be impacted by blame. Blame is bigger than that. In a study out of Stanford, researchers gave participants a news clip about a government official.[51] The excerpt one group was given showed the official blaming an organization for a mistake. The other group was given an excerpt showing the same official taking full responsibility for the same mistake.

Later on, both groups were prompted to write about a personal failure they had experienced. Even though they were given the same prompt, the two groups had drastically different responses. People who had just read about the government official blaming others were twice as likely to blame their own personal failure on somebody else.[51]

I'm sharing this information so you know some of the cognitive processes playing out when people practice naming and blaming. I'm also sharing so you can make informed decisions about *Who you want to be*.

How we think about our challenges matters. So does how we talk about them. This is more than semantics. It's science. And it influences which neural pathways and areas of the brain are activated.

There is one more study you should probably know about. Researchers found that people who practiced cognitive reframing saw significant affective improvements.[52] Their life-functioning and self-efficacy went up. While their depressive symptoms and perceived stress went down. Just by reframing events in a journal for two weeks.[52]

If you're unfamiliar with reframing, join the club. I used to confuse it with pretending problems didn't exist. So I wasn't a fan. However, I've come to learn reframing involves honestly acknowledging a situation. Then, trying to see the situation from a more positive, powerful, or growth-inducing perspective. The act of seeing something from an alternate perspective can change the meaning you associate with it. Which can help you change your thinking and response.[53]

Reframe with Caution

Some situations may not be appropriate to reframe. That's because they're so unhelpful, unhealthy, and problematic that reframing would detract from their true impact. More on this in a moment...

I was recently sitting on an airplane watching a Master Class by Malcolm Gladwell. He was explaining how medical professionals use something called a Kaplan-Meier analysis to compare the impact of certain treatments.[54] The analysis involves a basic plot graph with two lines. One line shows the survival rate of people on Treatment A. The second line shows the survival rate of people on Treatment B. The greater the separation between the lines, the bigger the difference one of the treatments is making.

Evidently, the Kaplan-Meier analysis is such a powerful visual, pharmaceutical companies will reveal the graph as a final slide when presenting research findings. Audiences have been known to burst into applause when they see even the slightest space between two lines because that space can represent millions of lives saved.

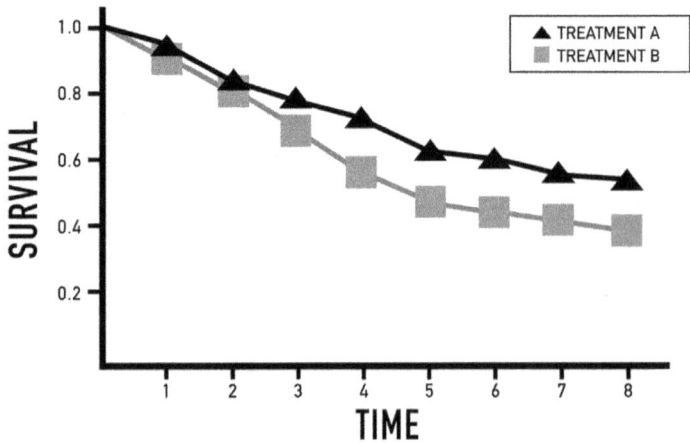

Figure 2.2: Hypothetical Kaplan-Meier graph

THE POWER OF "WHO YOU WANT TO BE"

I'm not a medical professional or statistician—and I'm definitely not Malcolm Gladwell. However, I created a completely fictitious Kaplan-Meier graph to show you how this works (see figure 2.2). Even I can see there is a significant space between the two hypothetical treatments. Therefore, you probably wouldn't want Treatment B.

I'm going to present some employee retention data next. It's real. Researchers analyzed the impact of 170 different causes of employee turnover in Culture 500 companies.[55] Each of these causes was then compared to employee compensation as a reference point.

Researchers found one thing that caused people to leave their jobs more than anything else. And when that one thing was compared to compensation, it wasn't even close. Which means it must have been a big deal. Because earning a paycheck that reflects the training, expertise, and difference you make is awfully important.

I took the liberty of converting this research into a Kaplan-Meier analysis. The graph I created compares the impact of compensation to the thing that causes people to quit more than anything else. While this data is from credible research, I don't think I've seen a Kaplan-Meier graph used in this way before, so it's on me if there are errors.

Try to notice the space between the two "treatments." It is an astonishing chasm. But *not* the kind people cheer for. Because it was created by a toxic culture. Toxic culture is the thing that is devastating people in Culture 500 companies and educators are not immune to it either.

Toxic culture is 10.4 times more likely to push a person to leave their position than the size of a paycheck (see figure 2.3).[55] Behaviors that are blatantly disrespectful, exclusionary, or antagonistic have real consequences. But so do some of the more subtle behaviors that can contribute to a toxic culture.

You and your team can determine what some of the less-prominent threats to culture in your school or context are. Just know that the slippery-slope effect is real. People are more prone to justify, excuse, or

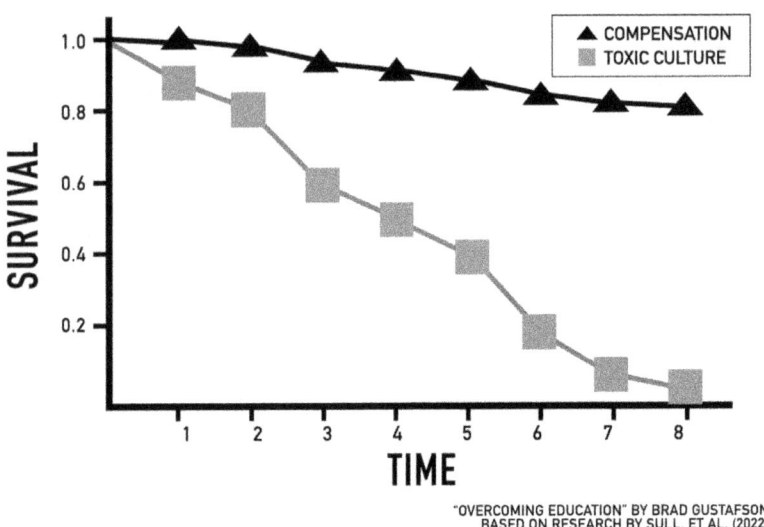

Figure 2.3: Toxic culture Kaplan-Meier graph

overlook smaller indiscretions than major ethical issues.[56] Over time, these behaviors add up.

> *Who you want to be* matters. But so does taking action on this decision. Because thought without action has consequences.

Moving from "What" to "Who"

I remember a time when I missed an opportunity to practice being *Who I want to be* as a leader. I was invited to meet with a team to go over some student-discipline issues. It was an important meeting to say the least. In the days leading up to the meeting, I found myself wondering what was going to be communicated to me, what I would say, and what we would do to address whatever was said. However, with all my

THE POWER OF "WHO YOU WANT TO BE"

worrying about the "whats," it didn't occur to me to think about *Who I wanted to be* going into that meeting.

When it was finally time to meet, we started by talking about all the whats. We named our challenges. I listened to how our challenges were impacting different areas of our work, including teachers' ability to teach, personal wellness, and the classroom environment. The teachers were incredible. But there was a point when I noticed something shift inside me.

I don't know if the team felt it, too. It might have been part way through our first meeting or midway through the second. (We needed a couple of meetings in order to give the issue the time it deserved.) The shift occurred after somebody suggested we invest some time into talking about *Who we wanted to be*. For students and each other. Here's the essence of what we decided:

We want to be people who...
- help students learn from mistakes
- show up with humanity and genuine care
- do not expect perfection
- are invested in the growth of our students
- hold students accountable using high expectations and necessary supports
- support authentic learning and change—not just saying, "sorry" without learning
- show up curious; seek to understand
- use our tools and apply our training (e.g., proactive teaching, Y-charts, basic needs)
- help students understand "non preferred tasks" are part of the human experience
- discipline in a dignified manner (e.g., avoid shaming and power struggles)

Our student-discipline issue did not evaporate just because we talked about *Who we wanted to be*. However, one of the things I noticed during our conversations was that articulating *Who we wanted to be* elevated our thinking. Therefore, it also helped us understand *Who we did **not** want to be*.

This story reminds me (a little bit) of the test-taking strategy of eliminating wrong answers in order to find the right one. However, there are not always right and wrong answers in this work we get to do. There are choices that move us closer to or further from *Who you want to be*.

Figure 2.4: How to move from what to who

One of the quickest ways to move from "what" to "who" is to pause. But you need to pause long enough for two things to happen. The first thing is to allow your worries, doubts, and endless supply of "whats" to fade away. Because then the second thing can start to happen. You give yourself a chance to decide *Who you want to be* (see figure 2.4).

> **Moving from "what" to "who" doesn't mean you ignore what's happening around you. It means you refuse to ignore the power inside you. It's never too late to shift from "what" to "who."**

How to Lead with "Who"

I promised you early on that I'd help you see the small and solvable aspects of bigger challenges. And I'm going to do the same with this super-fluency. Because leading with *"Who you want to be"* in mind is a very big deal. Deciding *Who you want to be* often starts with a question of some kind. You can access different aspects of your ideal self depending on whatever question you decide to reflect upon.

For example, when you ask, *"Who do I want to be when I'm talking about students, colleagues, or parents?"* you elevate how you talk about people when they're not in the same room as you.

When you ask, *"Who do I want to be when I notice certain systems aren't serving everyone?"* you can cultivate the courage needed to create more equitable and inclusive schools. There are many other things you could ask.

I put together several questions to help you in a variety of situations, including when you're framing challenges (see figure 2.5). The questions can be used with your team as well. To use the questions as a team, just change the word "I" to "we."

The more you and your team ask questions like these, the more likely you are to decrease the discrepancy between your actual and ideal selves. Here's a three-step process to help you move from simply deciding *Who you want to be* to taking action:

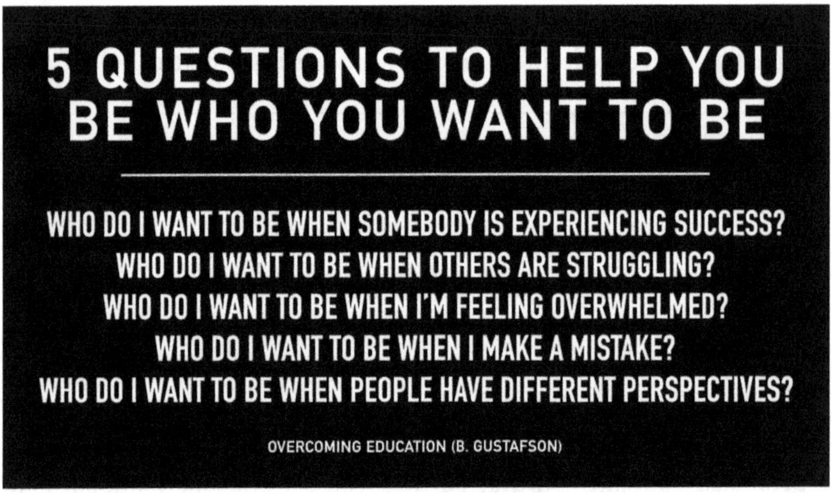

> **5 QUESTIONS TO HELP YOU BE WHO YOU WANT TO BE**
>
> WHO DO I WANT TO BE WHEN SOMEBODY IS EXPERIENCING SUCCESS?
> WHO DO I WANT TO BE WHEN OTHERS ARE STRUGGLING?
> WHO DO I WANT TO BE WHEN I'M FEELING OVERWHELMED?
> WHO DO I WANT TO BE WHEN I MAKE A MISTAKE?
> WHO DO I WANT TO BE WHEN PEOPLE HAVE DIFFERENT PERSPECTIVES?
>
> OVERCOMING EDUCATION (B. GUSTAFSON)

Figure 2.5: 5 questions to help...

1. Think about the question, *"Who do I want to be?"*
2. Name the next small step you could take to move closer to that version of yourself.
3. Then, do that thing. Take the step!

> You can leverage this super-fluency to make a difference in a variety of ways. It often starts with asking a question. But asking questions isn't enough. Being *Who you want to be* requires action.

Applying the Framework (Exercise)

We can't allow *Who we want to be* to remain a theoretical construct. Or something our students, team, and community catch a random glimpse of every few months. At some point *Who you want to be* needs to flow

THE POWER OF "WHO YOU WANT TO BE"

through your Mindsets, Communication, Priorities, and Actions. So that it can connect with your challenges and elevate outcomes. If this connection is never made, deciding *Who you want to be* could turn out to be the most irrelevant decision of your life.

This exercise will ensure that doesn't happen. It will help you cement the connection between the framework and your challenges—including *Who you want to be*.

OVERCOMING EDUCATION EXERCISE
APPLYING THE FRAMEWORK

HOW TO APPLY THE FRAMEWORK

DRAW OR DESCRIBE A CHALLENGE YOU'RE FACING IN THE SPACE ABOVE

Figure 2.6: How to apply the framework exercise

This exercise might seem simple. But this is by design. When it comes to making the connection between your challenges and the framework, you want it to feel intuitive. However, if you're a visual learner (like me) you may want to watch the short video on my website* that shows you how to apply the framework.

In the future, you'll probably want to make these connections mentally. However, I've found that people often appreciate a tactile connection using paper and pen the first time though. So here goes!

1. First, draw or describe a challenge you're facing in the blank space above (see figure 2.6). There's no wrong way to do this. (Our school recently experienced some flooding, so if I were completing this step I might describe the flooding or take a picture and use that for this exercise.)
2. Next, add a rudimentary sketch of the 5-Fluency Framework on top of what you just wrote. In case it's helpful, you can reference the framework found in the Introduction of this book (figure 0.3) to help you with this step. I recommend using a heavier pen or permanent marker. This will help the framework pop when it's drawn on top of the challenge you drew or wrote about in the first step.
3. Then, choose a fluency to focus on. I'd encourage you to consider choosing *Who you want to be* since that's the fluency we've been focusing on. But you do you.
4. Finally, think about how the fluency you chose connects to your challenge. What would it look, sound, and feel like to make an impact using only that fluency? If you had to name the smallest-possible step you could take using that fluency, what would it be?

---

* *The short video showing how to apply the framework to your challenges can be found on my website (BradGustafson.com). It also contains some additional commentary to walk you through this exercise — using an actual challenge I'm navigating.*

THE POWER OF "WHO YOU WANT TO BE"

> **I promised you that I'd help you learn to see the small and solvable parts hidden inside problems. Being able to connect *Who you want to be* to your challenges is an important part of how we're going to make this happen.**

Validating Doubt and Disbelief

If you're still unsure of how this is going to work, that's OK. It's OK if you have some serious doubts, too. Because I'm not going to ignore them. I compiled a couple of common forms of pushback people experience. Not just with this book, but with lots of things. Under each one is a thought, idea, or something I might say if we were discussing your pushback over a cup of coffee.

You could be thinking:
"This seems too simple to make a difference…"

If this is your concern, I appreciate your skepticism. It means you care about your time, work, and wanting to make a difference.

So here's the deal. Ease empowers impact. Many of the challenges you're facing are already complex. It's not helpful when the steps you're trying to take add to the chaos or create additional confusion. Over the course of this book, we'll go deeper into *how* and *why* each of the fluencies will help you make a difference. But they are intended to be accessible.

Or…
"This seems too hard or doesn't make sense yet…"

Connecting challenges to the fluencies and framework is a skill people develop. It is not something you either have or do not have. Give yourself grace if it's not making sense yet. If you're experiencing doubt or frustration along these lines, just know I'm committed to transforming the confusion into a more confident and equipped YOU by the end of the book.

Try to think about overcoming challenges like a giant jigsaw puzzle. Instead of trying to solve an entire 1,000-piece puzzle all at once, it helps to sort the pieces. The fluencies are a way to make sense of all the pieces.

Growing Forward

We all have the chance to decide *Who we want to be*. But not everyone approaches the decision with intention. Therefore, they never fully access the power at their core. But you are on your way to accessing this power.

Like a Banyan Tree that won't stop growing, the convictions you carry are capable of inspiring growth and new life. As Sojourner Truth demonstrated, small and consistent steps reveal *Who you want to be*. They can also change everything. But you must recognize the power you hold inside.

Education can be overwhelming. But making a difference doesn't have to be. Overcoming is a skill. Therefore, you can practice it. The next chapter is dedicated to helping you do just that. I'll show you how to apply *Who you want to be* to one of the most misunderstood fluencies of all: Mindsets. So that you can unlock and unleash the power inside you before taking action.

CHAPTER 3

Mindsets: How to Whisper with More Wolves

I have some good news. The time and thinking you invested into reading Chapter 2 is going to pay dividends here. I'm going to name a couple of common misconceptions about mindsets that many of us have been taught. I'll also share some strategies to help you create powerful mental structures. So you and your team can approach challenges with more mental agility and a higher capacity to overcome. Let's roll!

The Things People Think

People think about a lot of things. We think so much that 46.9% of the time we're doing something, we're thinking about something else.[57] We think about what other people are thinking. We even think about how many times they're thinking it.

I won't go into the weeds on this. But studies have even been done to determine the number of times the average human thinks about things like food, sleep, and sex each day.[58] I'm going to share some numbers for us to think about.

6,000+

Researchers discovered people have over 6,000 thoughts each day.[59] By using brain imaging scans, they documented an average of 6.5 thought transitions per minute. However, many of our thoughts 'worm' into others which makes them harder to detect. This might explain why some experts estimate we have between 50,000 to 80,000 thoughts each day![60, 61]

95%

We do a lot of thinking—that much is true. Which might explain why a whopping 95% of people believe they are self-aware![62] That's almost everyone! That number comes from a comprehensive study that spanned four years, included ten separate investigations, and involved nearly 5,000 participants.

10 - 15%

As it turns out, self-awareness is not as common as we think. Researchers found only 10-15% of people met the criteria for being self-aware.[62] Which means the majority of people think they are self-aware but aren't.

There are two kinds of self-awareness. And just because you're skilled in one doesn't necessarily mean you will be in the other.[63] Internal self-awareness involves how clearly you see your own thoughts, emotions, and aspirations (i.e., *Who you want to be*). External self-awareness involves an understanding of how others view these things in you. Evidently, a large majority of us are not as aware* as we think.

---

* *Self-awareness matters. Leaders who are able to see themselves as their co-workers and colleagues do, are viewed as more effective by those around them. They tend to have stronger relationships too.[63]*

The good news is—if you're one of the 85-90% of people who are not self aware—you don't have to stay stuck. This chapter will help you and your team bring additional intention to your thinking. I'll help you develop mental structures and hone some of your habits of mind. But I'll also help you cultivate a more adaptable mindset by learning how to cultivate and access different mindsets.

And in the off chance you're among the 10-15% of humans who are already self-aware, this chapter will provide you with additional strategies and mental structures to reinforce *Who you want to be*.

> **We come to work thinking. We think while we're at work. We even think about work after we've left. But all of this thinking may not be working for us—at least not as well as it could be. Therefore, we're going to look at mindset in a little different light.**

Validating Doubt and Disbelief

Before we go any further, I want to pause and acknowledge something. There has been a big focus on mindset in education the past several years. Certain concepts are almost ubiquitous.

Which means you could be thinking:
"I've already tried this…" or *"We already know about mindset…"*

Of course, there could be other things you're thinking, too. Like, *Is he really going to try and tell me about mindset?* Believe me, I would have been thinking a lot worse a few years ago. My biggest hang up with mindset was how it sometimes felt like it was being used against us. For example, it seemed like the message to educators was that instead of expecting reasonable resources and support from the system, we just needed to think more positively.

First, this chapter is not about telling you to be more positive. Second, I understand that many of us come to this work with all sorts of training and experiences with mindset. Therefore, I'll do my best to not repeat the things many of us have heard multiple times. I will also challenge a couple of things we might be getting wrong when it comes to mindset. So that when you finish this chapter you will have a more nuanced understanding of how you can access this fluency.

Or you might be thinking…
"I shouldn't have to read (or reread) anything on mindset…
I just need my supervisor or school to provide
support that's actually supportive…"

I'm going to write directly to those of you serving in formal leadership roles here. Therefore, if you're a principal, superintendent, or anybody else with keys that open more than one door in a building (metaphorically speaking) this next paragraph is for you.

As leaders, we have a responsibility to support people in ways that are meaningful to them. Mindset is clearly important. But teachers should not have to bear the weight of solving all of education's problems. Yet, many educators are feeling disrespected, under-supported, and unable to put their trust in us. We must step up to the plate and create conditions and systems that empower teachers to do their best work and thinking without burning out. For as much as mindset matters, so does tangible and responsive support from leadership.

A Cosmic Catapult

It can be helpful to think about a thing by taking a step back. So that's what I'm going to invite you to do. Instead of looking at mindset as a concept linked to your students, job, or trying to convince yourself that training for a marathon is fun, we're going to step back. Way back.

A lot has changed since 1969. If that first moon landing was "...a giant leap for mankind," the goal to create a settlement on Mars should be considered a cosmic catapult. The private sector has emerged as a force in the aerospace industry. Each new company brings even more astounding aspirations, from suborbital space tourism to pursuing interplanetary life.

In 2020, SpaceX became the first private company to send astronauts to the International Space Station.[64] Founded by Elon Musk, SpaceX's reusable Falcon 9 rockets have been the company's secret sauce. Reusing the most expensive parts of a rocket have resulted in more than 200+ reflights, tighter turnaround trips, and a $180 billion valuation.[65, 66]

If you're starting to think interplanetary living might be possible someday, you're not alone. But before we assume building a settlement on Mars is a foregone conclusion, it's important to consider the scale of this endeavor. The moon is less than 300,000 miles away–238,855 to be exact.[67] This number might sound big compared to your last road trip. However, if you round the distance to the nearest million miles, you'd be at zero. To put this in road-trip terms, it only takes three days to travel from Earth to the moon.[67]

On the other hand, Mars is around 140,000,000 miles away on average.[68] It takes approximately nine months to travel from Earth to the Red Planet.[68] A spacecraft's speed, distance, and the planet's position relative to Earth will impact how long the trip actually takes.

Astronauts and engineers must account for an infinite number of variables on a scale that's difficult to fathom. All this complexity makes me think about the thought process of the people involved in these missions. They're making a large number of complex decisions–somewhat similar to you and me. Which is the connection I wanted us to think about. Therefore, we're going to leave Mars and zoom back in again.

Earlier in this book, I shared the Jam Stand experiment with you. If you recall, that research discussed four ways people respond when they have too many choices.[69] I want to circle back to those four responses. But this time when you read the common ways people respond to having too many choices—try not to think about choosing your favorite flavor of jam. Instead, try to think about each response in terms of choosing your mindset.

Ways to approach choosing your mindset:
1. Defer the decision
2. Search for additional options
3. Choose the default option
4. Simply opt not to choose

I am sure there are instances when each of the four approaches to choosing your mindset might serve a strategic purpose. However, one of these approaches will ensure you unlock new ways of thinking. The others will not.

Searching for additional mindsets will strengthen your mental posture and agility. The more mindsets you have access to, the more adaptive your thinking can be.

Mental Postures

I like to think of mindsets in terms of your mental posture towards something. Your mental posture isn't just an internal construct. It can impact how others experience you. (Similar to how your mom might respond when she sees you slouching.) Therefore, choosing your mental posture is important for several reasons.

The problem is, many of us make this decision by default. Or we make a choice without understanding the options. This is more common than you might imagine. For whatever reason, we tend to think in terms of having either a growth or fixed mindset, without considering the multitude of other mindsets we have access to. But reducing mindset to two options restricts your mental flexibility, which weakens your mental posture.

Imagine if we viewed our physical posture as a binary decision: standing up straight or slouching. We'd have to ignore all the other ways people can physically show up and interact with their environment. Postures like sitting, kneeling, and laying down wouldn't be considered. Not to mention more nuanced physical postures that convey things like welcoming, curiosity, or defensiveness.

Yet, many of us talk about mindset in terms of there being an extremely limited number of options. Growth mindset is mentioned so frequently that we mistake it for the "correct" mindset. To be clear, believing you can grow through a combination of practice, effort, and learning from failure is not a bad thing.[70] However, we're not doing ourselves any favors when it's the only mindset we talk about. Or when we talk about it incorrectly (this happens!). But don't just take my word for it.

According to the psychologist who introduced the concept of growth mindset, many of us are getting it wrong. So badly that Carol Dweck says she's losing sleep over it. She calls the misuse of the concept "false growth mindset."[71] Dweck says it happens when people conflate effort, open mindedness, or any other good thing with a growth mindset itself. Positive personality traits can be helpful, but they are not the same as a growth mindset. A growth mindset is a life-long journey.[71] I would add that it is also one of many mental postures.

An example of a false growth mindset can be found in how we tend to overemphasize the role of effort (e.g., "Keep trying…don't give up") without teaching students the necessary skills, strategies, and habits of thinking that ensure learning.[72] Dweck has shared how her research on growth-mindset was intended to help close persistent gaps in achievement, not hide those gaps.[71] Effort should not supersede trying an alternate approach, asking for help, and actually learning.[73] Which is where the importance of having a strong and adaptable mental posture comes in.

When you encounter a challenge, you are likely to experience a variety of emotions. This is part of the human condition. But a big part of your internal response flows from your mental posture. Therefore, you do not want to limit yourself to one or two mindsets.

Mindsets as Actions of Thought

I've heard people say, "Actions speak louder than words." It makes sense. Actions inspire trust in a way words cannot. However, we should not underestimate the link between our thoughts and actions. Here's how I like to think about it…**Actions speak louder than words. But your thoughts whisper the script.**

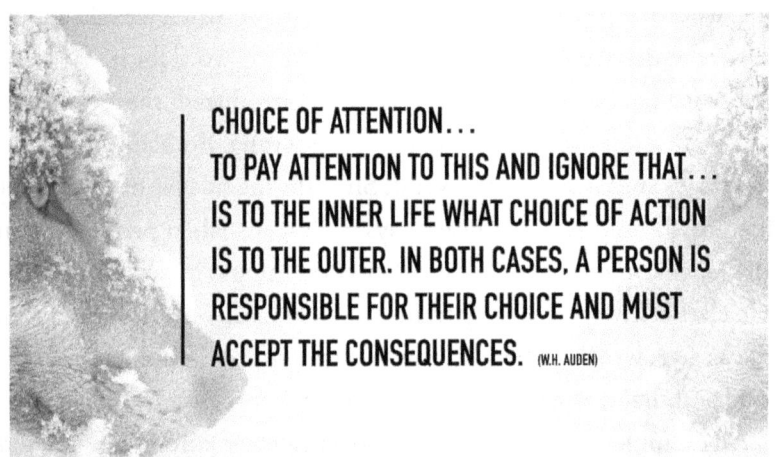

Figure 3.1: Choice of attention quote

There's a quote by W.H. Auden that frames the significance of thinking more effectively than anything else I've read. He refers to your focus as inner action (see figure 3.1). Therefore, I don't think it's too big a leap for us to consider mindsets as actions of thought.

But here's the problem—or at least one of them. There's this thing standing in the way. It's called the action bias.[74] It is a cognitive bias that makes it harder for people to attach value to the inner world of thought. Action bias can cause us to spend more time on observable decisions than those decisions that are more difficult for others to see. You might relate to the following example of social proof–or know somebody who does.

Some people spend more time deciding what they'll wear in the morning than choosing their mindset. One study found that over the course of a lifetime, some people spend close to a year deciding what to wear–287 days to be exact.[75] To be clear, this data doesn't represent everyone. It is connected to a sample of the population that responded to a survey. But in full transparency, there are many days where I'm sure I give more time to choosing which shoes to wear than the mindset I'm going to bring to work.

The action bias can also cause people to overvalue action and undervalue taking time to think things through.[74] One way to overcome this bias is to think about choosing your mindsets as an inner action. When you look at the 5-Fluency Framework, do not look at mindsets in isolation. Try to see them as being linked to actions (see figure 3.2).

Figure 3.2: Mindsets are actions of thought

The Power of Thinking Differently

A person's mindset can limit their options or unlock new and novel thinking. For example, a conventional mindset might push somebody to just try harder when faced with complex challenges—like trying to navigate the extreme conditions on the surface of Mars. The rovers we send to Mars encounter harsh temperatures, solar radiation, and a lot of dust. To the best of my knowledge, there are no Valvoline Instant Oil Changes, Tires Plus stores, or mechanics on Mars. (At least not yet.) This is an issue.

In 2014, the wheels on the Mars Curiosity rover were in rough shape.[76] Harsh winds and jagged rocks were contributing to a collection of dents and dings in the wheels. The team considered finding a more rover-friendly route to get Curiosity to its destination. But realistically speaking, there wasn't an easier route. It was Mars. So they decided to think differently about the situation instead, which required them to access a more innovative mindset.

The engineers knew some damage to the rover's six wheels was unavoidable, but they had to find a way to slow down the rate at which the tires were deteriorating. So the team tried driving the one-ton rover backwards.* Success!

A similar backwards-driving strategy had been used successfully almost a decade earlier when the Mars Opportunity rover ran into issues with its right-front wheel.[77] That team extended the life of Opportunity Rover's front wheels by driving backwards as well. Which led to Opportunity becoming the number one rover in the world for total distance traveled.

Nobody knows for sure how soon the tires of these rovers would have failed without the mind shift made by NASA engineers. Don't get

---

* *The Curiosity rover had only traveled 3.24 miles before needing to test its backward-driving capabilities. Thanks — in part — to the team's divergent thinking and backwards driving, the rover eventually put on a total of 16.2 miles before dying.*[76]

me wrong. Conventional thinking can serve a purpose. But the ability to access additional mindsets can help you and your team unlock new levels of potential.

Leaning heavily on a single mindset might be the opposite thing your challenges require. Pushing forward with the same mental posture that you've always done things with is not necessarily a strategy for overcoming.

However, taking a step back to relook at the things within your control is. The ability to shift mindsets is a small thing when compared to all the outward actions we can be biased towards. But this small thing can make a big difference.

In order to excel at thinking differently, we need to develop a more nuanced understanding of mindsets. Including how they work. How they don't work. And mostly, how to access more than one of them. Therefore, that's what we're going to explore.

The Wolves We Befriend

A few years ago, I was struggling with something work-related. I remember being at home, but not really being there—at least not mentally. My mind was consumed with a tricky situation. So I had slipped into replaying that situation in my mind over and over. One of my daughters shared the perfect encouragement with me in the form of a story. I had heard it before. But the fact my daughter shared it when I was stuck doing what the story says not to do made it especially meaningful. The origins of the story are unclear, but it has been attributed to the Cherokee. You may have heard it before too.

The Tale of Two Wolves

One evening an old Cherokee told his grandson about a battle that goes on inside people. He said, "My Son, the battle is between two wolves inside us all.

One is Evil. It is anger, envy, jealousy, doubt, sorrow, regret, greed, arrogance, self-pity, guilt, resentment, inferiority, lies, false pride, superiority, and ego.

The other is Good. It is joy, peace, love, hope, serenity, humility, kindness, benevolence, empathy, generosity, forgiveness, truth, compassion, and faith."

The grandson thought about it for a minute and then asked his grandfather: "Which wolf wins?"

The old Cherokee simply replied, "The one you feed."

I want to invite you to think about this story a little differently than you probably have before—assuming you have heard it before. But first, I want to respectfully acknowledge the diversity of Native American cultures.

I mentioned this story has been attributed to the Cherokee, but each community and culture has unique beliefs. Therefore, a single story should not be used to represent the values and beliefs of any Native American group. With this in mind, here's how I see this story helping us strengthen our mental posture.

Mindsets are often paired with an inverse mindset to help people draw distinctions between the two—just like in the story. Having a Positive Mindset vs. Negative Mindset is one of the more commonly referenced mindset pairings. A few of the other mindsets that have been paired together include:[78]

- Growth Mindset vs. Fixed Mindset
- Outcome Mindset vs. Process Mindset
- Abundance Mindset vs. Scarcity Mindset
- Entrepreneurial Mindset vs. Risk-Averse Mindset

MINDSETS: HOW TO WHISPER WITH MORE WOLVES

- Externally-Controlled Mindset vs. Internally-Controlled Mindset
- Individual Mindset vs. Collective Mindset
- Thinking Mindset vs. Feeling Mindset
- And many more...

One message I always take away from the story of two wolves is to be intentional with befriending the positive wolf. But I think there's more to it than that. More than one hundred mindsets have been documented over the years.[79] Instead of thinking about this story in terms of only having two wolves to choose from, I'd invite you to think about having access to an entire pack of wolves. We'll come back to this.

Anna Muzychuk

The term cognitive dissonance refers to a feeling of mental discomfort. It can be caused by conflicting attitudes, behaviors, or when somebody changes the location of a meeting at the last minute without telling you.[80] But cognitive dissonance can also be caused by changing your mind.

Anna Muzychuk is a highly-decorated chess grandmaster and former holder of two world-champion chess titles. In 2017, she lost both her titles—without being beaten. The tournament where she was supposed to defend her titles was being played in Saudi Arabia where women do not have the same rights as men.[81] In the days leading up to the tournament, Muzychuk shared a message on social media stating she did not want to be treated like a "secondary creature." Therefore, she would not be attending the tournament. Many people applauded her for staying true to her principles. But not everyone.

Some people pointed out how Muzychuk had participated in a previous tournament in Iran where she experienced similar restrictions. Muzychuk responded to the criticism by explaining that her previous experience helped inform her decision not to play in Saudi Arabia.[81]

There will always be people who try to tell you who you are. Or who you were. But you are not your past decisions. You have a right to change your mind—especially when you have new information. You're the only one who gets to decide *Who you want to be*.

There are aspects of life we'd all like a do-over on. I've never shared this before—with anyone. I quit drinking alcohol more than a decade ago. It's probably getting closer to fifteen years now. I don't remember the exact date or year. But I do know that drinking had become more than a casual endeavor for me. It was quietly influencing how I would approach social decisions. If given the choice to hang out where alcohol was an option, that would have been my choice.

In some ways, drinking had also become the glue keeping many of my relationships outside of work going. To be clear, this was a reflection on me, nobody else. But I'm sharing this because it's the most authentic way I can explain how a person's thinking can change.

Again, I'm not judging anyone. Especially if you have a healthy relationship with alcohol. That just wasn't me. I don't want to go too far into the weeds on this, but I also want to be honest that making this change was not easy. I don't think I could have done it without a healthy dose of prayer and the power of Jesus.

With all this said, I'm guessing there were friends who may have struggled with my decision. Changing my mental posture towards drinking meant I needed to make additional decisions about how and where I spent my free time. Therefore, I started seeing less of some incredible people and friends who I care a great deal about.

> **Changing your mind and expanding your thinking is not always easy. It can involve cognitive dissonance. But working through the mental discomfort in pursuit of *Who you want to be* is a growth-inducing process.**

Exploring Mindsets (Exercise)

I remember visiting a colleague's classroom early in my career. I was only in my 2nd or 3rd year teaching. I don't recall what I was needing help with. Probably everything. But I'll never forget this colleague gesturing to a sheet of paper on the wall next to her desk. It was a Charles Swindoll quote about attitude (see figure 3.3). It is a sheet of paper I still think about 20+ years later.

> **Attitude by Charles Swindoll**
>
> "The longer I live, the more I realize the impact of attitude on life.
>
> Attitude, to me, is more important than facts. It is more important than the past, than education, than money, than circumstances, than failures, than successes, than what other people think, say or do. It is more important than appearance, giftedness or skill…
>
> The remarkable thing is we have a choice every day regarding the attitude we embrace for that day."

Figure 3.3: Charles Swindoll quote about attitude

Maybe it was the unassuming way in which she drew my attention to the quote. Or maybe it was what the words stirred inside me. But that was the day I decided to be more intentional with my mindset.

I haven't had too many clarion moments like that in my life. However, I recently had another one. I was reading an article by Steven Burns about mindset.[78] The article mentioned that many people lean heavily on one mindset. What we might not realize is that we have a mixture of many mindsets inside us.

This got me thinking about all the circumstances an educator navigates over the course of a day and how helpful it could be to access the right mindset for the moment. But the ability to change your mindset is more than just helpful. It's a skill. And navigating complex challenges requires this skill. Therefore, I'm going to help you practice and develop it.

OVERCOMING EDUCATION EXERCISE
EXPLORING MINDSETS

For this exercise, I want to invite you to think about mindsets as mental structures. Specifically triangles. Because we want to build strong mental structures and triangles are known for their strength.*

1. First, brainstorm some of the mindsets you might like to explore (see figure 3.4). Write them down on the lines. But don't worry about whether the words you write are official mindsets. You could write down any attitude, belief, or habit of thinking that you might like to explore.
2. Next, reread the words you wrote on the lines. Choose three

---

* *When force is applied to a triangle, a combination of stretching and compression occurs. Therefore, engineers will design structures—like bridges and roofs—using triangles because of the large amount of weight the shape can hold.*[82]

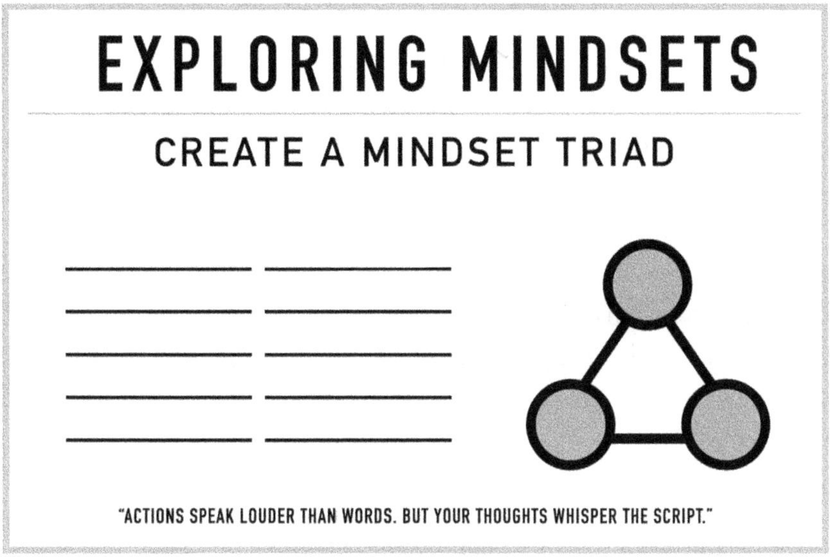

MINDSETS: HOW TO WHISPER WITH MORE WOLVES

EXPLORING MINDSETS

CREATE A MINDSET TRIAD

"ACTIONS SPEAK LOUDER THAN WORDS. BUT YOUR THOUGHTS WHISPER THE SCRIPT."

Figure 3.4: Exploring mindsets – create a mindset triad

to focus on and circle those three words. Try to select a combination of words that will inspire, challenge, and stretch your thinking.

3. Then, write the three words you selected in the shaded circles or nearby each circle (see figure 3.4). All done? Congratulations! You've just created a mindset triad!
4. Finally, practice using it. To access the power of a mindset triad, try to look at a situation through the lens of one of the mindsets in your triad. After that, change lenses. Try looking at the same situation using one of the other mindsets in your triad.

In my role as principal, one of the mindset triads that I often access includes Growth Mindset, Systems-Thinking, and Smalvable (i.e., Small and Solvable). Rotating between these three mindsets has helped me have a more nimble mental posture. It also provides some context to the promise I made to you earlier in this book. When I committed to helping you see the small and solvable things in larger problems, I knew you'd need to develop a mental posture that's inclined to look for things within your control.

Ideally, you would work your way up to carrying multiple mindset triads throughout the day. However, I'd suggest starting with one. There's a good chance you already possess several well-established beliefs. You might just need to be more intentional with how you're accessing them.

The Daily Aspiration

Flexibly shifting between mindsets can be helpful. But there may be times when you need one quick and reliable word in order to access your ideal self during a meeting, student meltdown, or when you're interacting with a supervisor who has toxic tendencies. Therefore, I'm going to show you a simple mental structure that can be used on its own or along with the mindset triad you just created (see figure 3.5). I call it the daily aspiration.

A daily aspiration is a word you decide to carry throughout the day. I used the word "joy" in the example below. When I choose joy as my daily aspiration, I'm more intentional about finding joy and protecting my inner joy.

But the daily aspiration also helps me share my joy with others. A few of my other go-to daily aspirations include words like calm, gratitude, and listen.

The key is to reflect upon whatever word you choose throughout the day. Celebrate when you're walking in your purpose and carrying this word well. Notice when you're drifting from *Who you want to be* (e.g., when you're losing your patience with a student or colleague).

When this happens, gently remind yourself of your daily aspiration and try to reset with that word in mind.

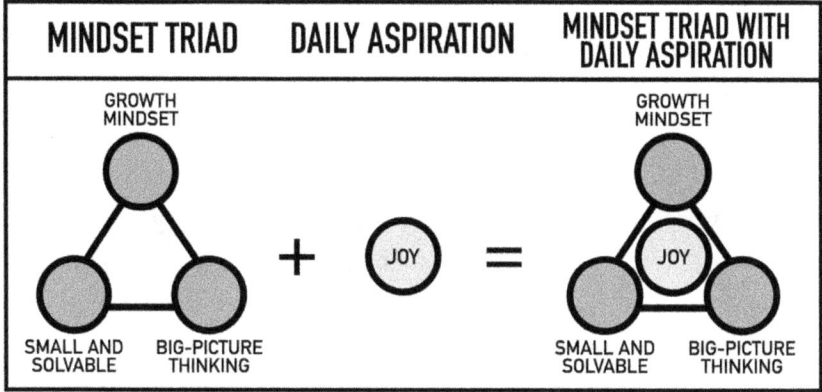

Figure 3.5: Combining mental structures

To be clear, you do not need to combine your daily aspiration with anything else. It is powerful on its own. The daily aspiration is one of the primary mental structures I use when entering into difficult conversations, complex challenges, or when I'm just plain struggling. This practical strategy aligns with the core message of this book. Education can be challenging. But making a difference doesn't have to be.

> Enhancing your mental posture doesn't take a lot of time.
> But it does require intention. Only you can decide
> *Who you want to be.* And only you know what mindsets
> and mental structures will work for you.

Poisoned Pawns

Building strong, adaptable mental structures is important. But so is avoiding mind traps that will poison your thinking. Therefore, I'm going to point out one of these mind traps—using an analogy that chess grandmaster Anna Muzychuk might appreciate.

In chess, a poisoned pawn refers to a tactical maneuver where a player leaves a pawn unprotected—or at least that's how it might appear to their opponent. But capturing the poisoned pawn requires an opponent to give up positional advantage or lose one of their pieces in the exchange.[83]

I'm not a chess grandmaster.* But everything I've read about the different variations of poisoned pawns tells me they are a gambit beginners should avoid. The problem is, nobody warns you if a pawn happens to be poisoned. You must be on the lookout for them.

Chess is not the only time quick wins can be accompanied by hidden costs. Playing the blame game is a lot like capturing a poison pawn. Blame might feel like a quick win, but pointing the finger at somebody else comes with a cost. I mentioned in the previous chapter how blame triggers the part of the brain that activates a fight, flight, or freeze response.[84] But, it can also impact your reputation, relationships, and quietly erode the culture you're trying to create. I tend to believe there's a better move, and I'm going to show it to you. I call it "The Candy Cane." It's a practical strategy you can use today. It's also the quickest way to avoid falling prey to a poisoned pawn. To practice using The Candy Cane, try following these three steps:

1. Extend your arm straight out in front of you.
2. Point your finger straight out.
3. Curl the end of your pointer finger back towards yourself so your arm and finger form a candy cane shape.

---

* In addition to not being a chess Grandmaster, I suffered a devastating loss in the one and only chess tournament I was ever in. It happened in 6th grade. And it only took my opponent four moves to beat me. A feat I didn't even know was possible until that fateful day.

MINDSETS: HOW TO WHISPER WITH MORE WOLVES

If you followed the three steps correctly, you should now be pointing at yourself. I will occasionally use the candy cane in meetings, complete with the arm motion. It helps me verbalize *Who I want to be*. But it also shows people the one person each of us can control in tricky situations.

> The candy cane can become a mindset if you practice it enough. No matter how challenging a situation or behavior might be, you always get to choose *Who you want to be* and how you'll respond.

No More Flat Tires

Being intentional with one mindset can make a difference. But being able to access multiple mindsets will empower you and your team to move forward on your most ambitious goals.

I imagine that even NASA's engineers feel deflated at times. Mars is a cold and unforgiving terrain. Therefore, trying to develop a rover tire capable of withstanding that environment can't be easy, especially given the track record of previous tire designs (and failures). But NASA engineers have been able to adapt and overcome.

They've made major breakthroughs in tire technology.[85, 86] The team at NASA's Glenn Research Center have engineered a tire using shape-shifting materials. The tires appear to be made from thousands of coils. The coils don't require air and can flex around rocks instead of being punctured by them.

I want to share a few mindsets I noticed when reviewing online interviews and research on the design process. As a disclaimer, engineers didn't announce when they were shifting their thinking during interviews. I'm simply sharing a few of the different mindsets I noticed engineers accessing.

Entrepreneurial Mindset: The engineers were not limited by materials and thinking they had used in the past. They leveraged creativity and innovation.

Growth Mindset: The engineers did not just try harder using the same approach. They learned from their failures, developed a deeper understanding of their problems, and tested different approaches.

Scarcity Mindset: This mindset is the inverse of an Abundance mindset, but that doesn't mean it's bad. The engineers were realistic about the limitations of Mars. Resources and opportunities for repair on the Red Planet are scarce. Therefore, they needed to create a tire that fit within the constraints of the situation. (Sound familiar?!)

You can't unlock limitless potential with a single mindset. But accessing multiple mindsets is a skill. Therefore, you can practice it.

I've been emphasizing the power of creating mental structures that are more nimble and adaptable for most of this chapter. As an "Autism dad" and principal to many incredible and neurodiverse human beings, I also want to share a heartfelt plea. As you and your team forge new and powerful mindsets, please continue to think about students and colleagues who are neurodiverse.

What the world may see as detail-oriented, rigid, or any number of other labels, I see as my family and students. Be quick to notice the strengths and passions of others. And do what you can to make school feel a little less like it wasn't made for them. I'm not pretending to have the answer to this. But something tells me it involves *Who we want to be*, mindsets, and practicing the candy cane strategy I mentioned in the previous section.

MINDSETS: HOW TO WHISPER WITH MORE WOLVES

The Pack

Growing up as a teacher's kid had its perks. Every summer, my mom would bring her classroom computer home. Which meant I had unlimited access to playing "Oregon Trail" and "Word Munchers." Playing games on that pixelated black and green screen was fun. But nothing compared to getting to go with Mom to her school.

There were several summers when I got to hang out in my mom's classroom while she was either packing up from summer school or getting ready for the next school year. I don't remember everything about those visits, but I do remember a large banner that was prominently displayed in her classroom: *"The strength of the wolf is in the pack; the strength of the pack is in the wolf."*

I think I understand why my mom liked the quote. But I'm sharing it with you for a different reason. You can feed more than one wolf–and every wolf matters. With enough practice and intention, you can cultivate and access an entire pack. Creating mental structures–like mindset triads and using daily aspirations–will help, which is why I wanted to share my mom's quote with you. Having access to multiple mindsets is like always having a supportive pack of wolves on your side.

You have more than 6,000 thoughts everyday–don't leave them to chance! The challenges you and your team are facing are worthy of your best thinking. Therefore, it's important to develop strong and adaptable mental structures so you can whisper to the wolves that will empower you to innovate, collaborate, and overcome.

CHAPTER 4

Communication: How to Speak the Language of Connection

Many people think others need to improve their communication skills. But let's be honest: we all miscommunicate, under-communicate, and occasionally wish we didn't have to communicate with certain human beings. Yet, when we learn how to communicate more effectively, it helps *everything* go more smoothly.

This chapter dives into key aspects of communication that will help you speak the language of connection more fluently–starting with understanding how to make internal connections that build authenticity and trust. We'll also explore how to listen for the frequencies other people are using, so your efforts to make a difference are not misunderstood.

Lost in Translation

Some jobs require stronger communication skills than others. But have you ever thought about the professions in which communication might be the most critical?! Education, healthcare, and serving as the President of the United States come to mind.

Shortly after President Jimmy Carter left office, he was giving a speech in Japan.[87] In an effort to connect with his audience, he went off script and attempted to tell a joke. He knew the joke was not his best material; however, it was the best he could come up with at the time. He also knew that humor can be a powerful way to connect with an audience. So he went for it.

As the Japanese interpreter translated President Carter's joke, the audience responded with wild enthusiasm. They loved it. Based upon their approving laughter, it appeared President Carter had created an authentic connection with his audience.

However, something wasn't sitting right. President Carter knew the joke was not *that* good. He was also struggling with how quickly the interpreter had translated it. Curiosity drove President Carter to circle back to the translator. Which is when that person admitted to translating the joke as, "President Carter told a funny story. Everyone must laugh."

I'd assume a translator's primary responsibility is to communicate accurately. Especially when translating for a president who was well-respected for his knowledge, humor, and communication skills.*

But this story is not about blaming a translator. It's about accepting that you are the number one influence on how effective your communication is. I could share countless studies pointing to the importance of communication. But I'm not going to insult your intelligence. You already know communication is vital. Instead, I'm going to share a large

---

* *A researcher from UC Davis used factors like intellectual knowledge, humor, and receptiveness to estimate the intelligence of every former President. Carter came in near the top of the list with an impressive 156.8—well above an average I.Q., which hovers around 100 depending on the assessment used.*[88] *As an additional fun fact just for you, Carter's presidency produced the first cabinet-level Department of Education in 1980.*[89]

number with you. Then, I'm going to ask you to think about the role communication played (or didn't play) in making this number happen.

90%

Across all races, income, and education levels, 90% of all parents sincerely believe their child is at or above grade level.[90] That's nine out of ten families who somehow have the impression their child is meeting or exceeding the standards. I'm not sure where you work, but 90% of the students I get to work with each day are not at or above grade-level standards yet.

Unless I'm mistaken something has gotten lost in translation. It could be that families aren't paying attention. Or it could be that the connection we want to have with families is not as strong or clear as we want it to be yet. Either way, it's not only former Presidents of the United States who experience miscommunication.

You CAN'T control whether people read your email, newsletters, or open up their children's report cards. You CAN'T control how others interpret your words. But you CAN improve the skills you use to deliver them.

Effective communication is not easy. There are some aspects of communication that are outside your control. But focusing on those aspects will not make you a more effective communicator. Learning how to navigate challenging communication is in your control. It's also a skill. Therefore, you can practice it.

Quick-Response (Exercise)

In this chapter, we will look at some of the things you can do to communicate more effectively across multiple communication mediums, so you can navigate your challenges with increased confidence—even when it feels like communication is strained. This exercise will help you reflect on your beliefs about communication, which will help us build upon the strengths you already have.

OVERCOMING EDUCATION EXERCISE
QUICK-RESPONSE SCENARIO

Imagine you're at a workshop or professional conference. Before the first session, you find yourself waiting in line for a cup of coffee, water, or whatever you like to drink before a conference. There's another attendee in line next to you. You strike up a conversation and, before you know it, you're feeling a genuine sense of connection. (My fellow introverts might be eyeing the exit. But hang in there for a minute. The small talk is almost over.)

The other attendee is explaining how they love their work on most days. Working with kids is clearly a passion for them. However, they've been struggling to see eye-to-eye with a parent. At one point in the conversation they share a half smile and say, "Maybe it would be easier if I just stopped communicating."

You both laugh at this. But something tells you the comment is more of a plea for help than a joke. And now they're asking for your perspective. But they do not have a lot of time. Therefore, whatever you're about to say needs to be concise and precise—a quick and important response.

1. Take a second to think about what communication means to you. How does communication work? What might be missing when it's not working? Reflect on this.

2. Now, if you only have one or two quick sentences to share with this person, what would you say? In the space below, write what you think the essence of communication is…or any other perspective you can provide.

_____
_____
_____
_____.

To end this scenario, imagine yourself sharing your perspective with the educator. After listening to you, they smile and let you know that they plan on carrying your words with them for a long time. Then, they pay for your beverage before you go your separate ways. (So maybe it was worth sticking around?!)

We will revisit your thoughts on communication later in this chapter. If you completed this exercise mentally it might not hurt to jot down a sentence or two; that way you have something you can circle back to.

Communication as an Act of Connection

Communication can take many forms and serve many functions. It can influence, inform, and inspire—among many other things. I'm not advocating for one form or function of communication over any other. But I am going to help you think about the things we do that create confusion, unproductive conflict, and lead to a loss of trust—so that you can do less of those damaging things and spend more time making a difference.

Many people use the words "communicate" and "connect" interchangeably. But they are not the same. When somebody says they are going to try and *connect* with a parent, it sometimes means sending an email, leaving a voicemail, or secretly hoping no one answers the phone.

Similarly, when we say we're going to *connect* with a colleague, it can mean we're going to text or check-in with a co-worker. Unfortunately, none of these communication formats ensure the other person feels seen, heard, or experiences true *connection*.

In order to create *connection*, it helps to be connected. But I'm not talking about being connected to your professional network, social circle, or anything having to do with the strength of your Wi-Fi signal. The kind of *connection* I'm talking about is inside you.

It's something psychologists refer to as "attunement," which involves being aware of and responsive to a person's needs.[91] When you're attuned to yourself, you're more equipped to attune with others—even when no words are spoken.[92, 93] Therefore, I'm going to help you strengthen the degree to which your communication is connected internally (see figure 4.1) so that your ability to show up with authenticity, inspire trust, and attune to others increases as well.

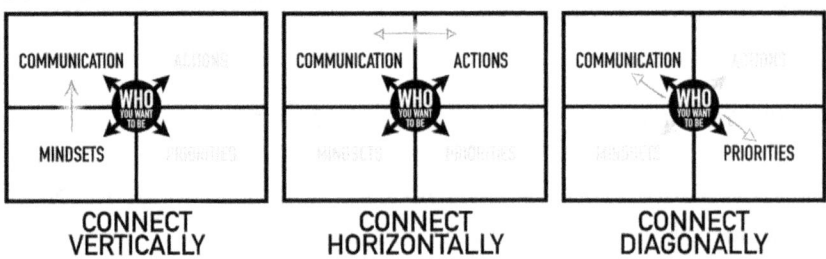

Figure 4.1: Connect internally to create connection with others

Over the next several pages, I'll share some examples of how communication can be connected internally, so that you give yourself a chance when trying to speak the language of *connection* with others. But I'll also make a case for why these internal connections matter in terms of psychology, neuroscience, and helping you resist the temptation of hitting "reply all" on district emails.

Connect Vertically

Your mindsets flow up and into your communication—whether you want them to or not (see figure 4.2). This flow inspires the words you speak. But it also creates authenticity. Therefore, not paying attention to it will impact the effectiveness of your communication.

This is especially true when you are feeling overwhelmed, undersupported, or facing complex challenges. When you're under stress, you are more susceptible to saying things you don't mean.[94]

Psychologists have studied what happens in the brain when people say hurtful things. When you're experiencing intense emotions your amygdala can become hyperactive and hijack your thinking. This can create fear, flashes of anger, or lead to you saying something that doesn't reflect your true thinking—at least not when you're in a more rational state of mind.

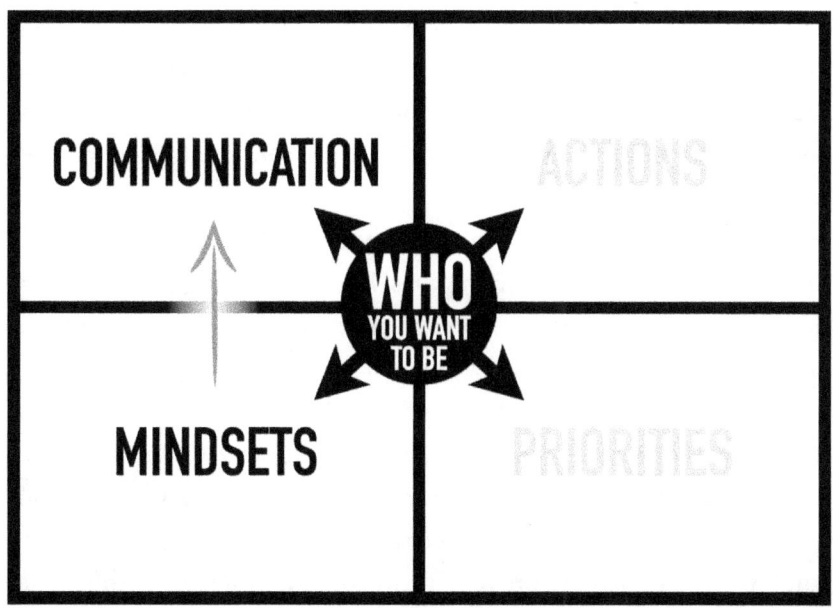

Figure 4.2: Vertical connection between communication and mindsets

I'm not proud to admit this, but I remember sitting in a meeting feeling bitter and defeated. My mindset was not in a productive place. The number of needs back at my school—as well as the intensity of those needs—was overwhelming. So I did not show up to this meeting as *Who I wanted to be*.

I don't remember what was being discussed. However, I do remember a thought that flashed through my mind: *These people are idiots.* I knew this line of thinking did not represent *Who I wanted to be*. It didn't represent how I actually felt when I was thinking rationally either. Because the people in that meeting were actually some of the most dedicated, focused, and hardworking people I know.

Thankfully, I took a moment to pause and observe the room. As I thought about each person individually, I reminded myself about their genuine care for students. Which helped me interrupt my own thinking.

The simple act of bringing intention to the vertical connection helped me move closer to *Who I wanted to be*. The reality was everyone in that meeting was just as committed to making a positive difference as I was. I had allowed my mindset to write an internal script that wasn't helpful to anyone, myself included. And my communication suffered as a result.

It wasn't exactly easy to share these thoughts with you—especially knowing how flawed my thinking was. But if I'm asking you to authentically reflect on how connected your mindset and communication is, I know I need to do the same. Even when it's messy.

Approaching communication with even the smallest awareness of this vertical connection can mean the difference between showing up as your authentic self or allowing your amygdala to hijack your communication. It can also help you understand what's happening in the brain when you or somebody on your team communicates something that doesn't reflect rational and authentic thinking.

Some experts in the field of psychology have ranked authenticity as one of the top three[*] needs people have.[95] Authenticity is correlated to improved mental health, well-being, and increased coping skills. (Sign me up for those please!)

I wish achieving authenticity was easier. But as far as I can tell, authenticity is not a destination. It is a dynamic journey that requires ongoing intention. Checking in with yourself. And noticing when you want to make adjustments to the vertical connection between communication and mindsets.

Psychologists continue to debate all the components of authenticity.[96] However, Michael Kernis and Brian Goldman identified self-awareness as a key ingredient in authenticity.[95] Self-awareness comes from reflecting on your motives, checking-in with your emotions, and thinking before, during, and after you communicate. By practicing this on a regular basis, you will be more equipped to bring your authentic self to your communication and challenges.

> Just remember, authenticity and self-awareness are not one-time events or checklist-type traits. We develop them by monitoring the flow between our mindsets and communication over time.

Connect Horizontally

A horizontal connection creates trust (see figure 4.3). But not just with other people. A strong horizontal connection can create self-trust.[97] Developing self-trust helps you communicate with more confidence and kindness, even if you're only speaking to yourself.

---

[*] *Authenticity has been described as a cornerstone to mental health. The other two top needs people have are relatedness (e.g., belonging or feeling loved) and competence.*[95]

Unfortunately, the opposite is also true. Your confidence can waver when the connection between your words and actions is inconsistent. And losing confidence in what you say and do can lead to carrying things like regret, shame, or the habit of hyper-focusing on your mistakes. This is not the kind of baggage you want to carry when you're trying to make a difference. **Belief from others can be a boost. But there's a quiet strength that comes from trusting yourself. Even as you experience doubt, overthinking, and the occasional breakdown.**

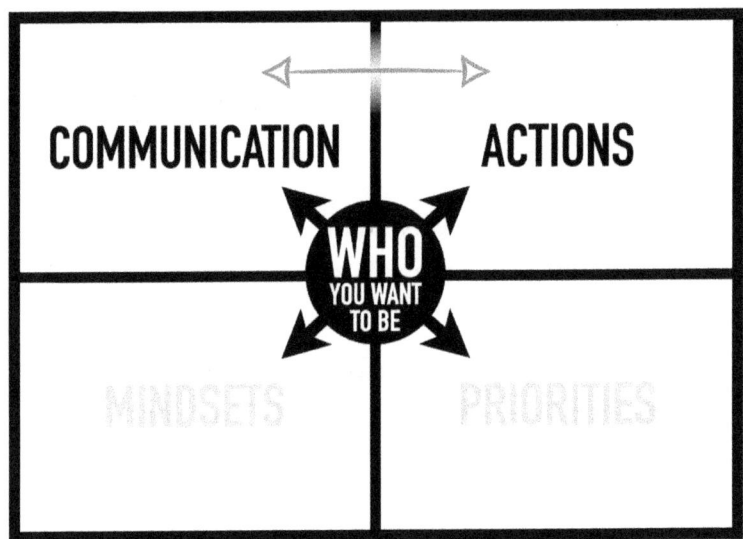

Figure 4.3: Horizontal connection between communication and actions

In case you're wondering (or nervous), self-trust doesn't mean everything you say and do has to be perfect. Being human disqualifies you from having that ability. However, enhancing the congruence between your communication and actions can increase your self-trust. I'm going to share a story that highlights the importance of tending to your horizontal connection. The story involves an interview I had a number of years ago. But it's not really about the interview. Instead, try to notice the different opportunities I had within the experience to practice self-trust.

I remember walking into an interview for my dream job. It was for an elementary principal position in a wonderful district that was relatively close to where my wife and I grew up. The interview process spanned a couple of weeks. However, one of the interview days involved me meeting with three different stakeholder groups: staff, students, and families.

The first rotation was with a large group of teachers in the school gymnasium. After spending 20-30 minutes answering questions with teachers, I rotated to an adjoining space where I met with families. I recall the questions the families asked me were similar to those that had been asked by teachers. However, I noticed families were emphasizing different aspects of the questions. It was subtle. But it seemed like they were wanting different answers than I had provided the teachers when it came to things like homework expectations, communication, and the level of involvement parents should have in decision-making.

Once I was done meeting with families, I was escorted to the media center for a third and final rotation with students. That was a lot of fun. Except for one student who kept asking how old I was—this was a question I hadn't practiced during my interview prep.

After the three interview rotations were complete, I managed to find my way back to the gym. A few teachers approached me to introduce themselves. As we were chatting, another teacher joined us. Unbeknownst to me, that teacher had rotated through all the interview stations. Therefore, this individual had a chance to hear how I responded to questions about things like parent communication, high-stakes testing, and student discipline in front of three very different audiences.

As I started to process this revelation, I remember being filled with a sense of peace. You could call it self-trust. I knew I had responded to the interview questions in each rotation with the same core values in mind. I may have used different stories and vocabulary to share *Who I wanted to be* with each group. But I was confident I had maintained an integrity of messaging throughout the entire process. Now, I'm having this epiphany.

> **Life is like a series of rotations. But instead of rotating between interview groups we're rotating between people, challenges, and experiences. Some of these experiences are joy-filled and others are unlike anything you would ever choose for yourself. However, every single experience is an opportunity to strengthen the connection between your communication and actions.**

Connect Diagonally

I shared a story about President Jimmy Carter and his interpreter at the beginning of this chapter. But I'm going to share a story from more recent history here. As you're reading, I'd encourage you to look past whatever political party each person is from. Instead, try to think about the connection between their communication and priorities–this is what the diagonal connection is all about!

On September 25, 2008, Barack Obama and John McCain were both actively campaigning to become president. This was also the same period that our country was experiencing an economic crisis.[98] The housing bubble had burst, and Obama and McCain were called to an emergency meeting with Congressional leaders.

President Bush opened the meeting and then turned to the Democratic House Speaker, Nancy Pelosi, for her remarks. However, she yielded the floor to Barack Obama, who had prepared to communicate. And communicate he did!

After that, President Bush turned to John McCain and extended the same opportunity to speak. However, things didn't go as well. After improvising for a couple of minutes, McCain reportedly fell silent. And so did everyone else. The connection between McCain's priorities and communication was not as clear as it could have been.

Later on, President Obama recalled the story and said, "There are moments in an election and life where all possible paths except one suddenly close. This was one of those moments."

We all have things that matter to us. But we also have moments when we don't communicate our priorities as well as we would have liked (see figure 4.4). I can relate.

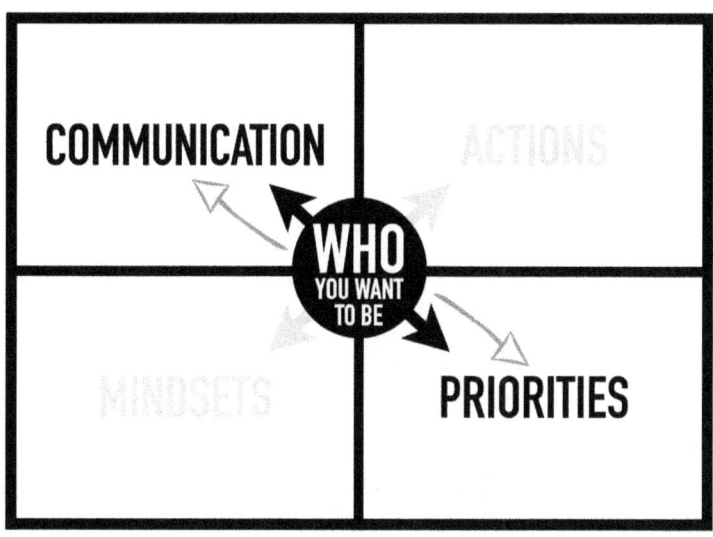

Figure 4.4: Diagonal connection between communication and priorities

There have been times when something was important to me. But I did not communicate clearly or consistently about that thing, which led to the priority being more clear and important to me than anyone else. This is not how a strong diagonal connection works.

The absence of communication (and under-communication) lead to frustration, disappointment, and friends ordering the worst-possible pizza toppings when we go to restaurants together. The power of shared priorities decreases when you don't talk about them clearly and consistently.

With this in mind, I want to share a strategy to help sharpen conversations about things that matter. However, it's not a new idea. It involves using stories to communicate priorities. Sharing a story or analogy can reveal the essence of a priority more than information alone. But here's the thing: sharing a story doesn't ensure everyone walks away with the same understanding.

Our brains are not very good at separating past experiences from new learning—even when the new information is introduced in the form of a compelling story.[98] That's because people apply their own meaning and interpretations to new information, including the stories they hear. These interpretations are based heavily on their own lived experiences.

The neuroscience behind this is fascinating. Our brains are hardwired to apply our own unique meaning to new information and stories. This means you and your team might hear the same story and walk away with a different understanding of what the priority is. However, you can overcome this tendency by providing people with a frame of reference before telling a story.[99]

You can do this by sharing a simple explanation for why you're sharing a story—before sharing it. (I've attempted to do this throughout this book.) Another option is to provide prompts or breadcrumbs that point people to what you want them to listen for. You could also front-load a story by sharing the take-away at the beginning.

> **By being more intentional with the internal connection between your communication and priorities, you (and your message!) are more likely to *connect* with others.**

Validating Doubt and Disbelief

I recognize communication often involves more than one person. That's one reason it's so tricky.

Therefore, you could be thinking:
"I will never be able to convince my team to do all this..." or
"I'm not even sure I can remember all these connections..."

The good news is you don't have to convince anyone of anything. You don't even have to remember it all yourself. The previous sections were designed to help you show up to conversations closer to *Who you want to be*. Instead of trying to remember all the internal connections every time you communicate, I'd suggest picking one to focus on for a period of time. Perhaps after experiencing some growth and success with one of these internal connections, you'll feel differently about sharing with your team. If not, that's OK, too.

Frequencies, Feelings, and Failing to Connect

Up to this point, we've focused on connecting internally, with the understanding that internal connectedness will help you create *connection* with others. But no matter how connected you are internally, you cannot assume others will be on the same wavelength as you. It's actually safer to assume they are not on your wavelength.

Somewhere in the north Pacific Ocean there's a whale that's baffled the scientific community for nearly three decades. Some have said it's the loneliest whale in the world.[100] Most whales communicate by making a series of low-frequency vocalizations. They make noises that are anywhere between 15 - 30 Hertz (Hz) and capable of traveling thousands of miles through the ocean.[100] But the loneliest whale's vocalizations are around 52 Hz. For whatever reason, the loneliest whale communicates on a completely different frequency than other whales (see figure 4.5).

Figure 4.5: The loneliest whale

Many scientists believe the loneliest whale has lived its entire life without being heard by other whales.[100] Some scientists have speculated other whales might be able to hear the loneliest whale. But they think the loneliest whale's high-pitched vocalizations probably sound more like an inaudible helium voice to other whales. However, this isn't really a story about whale vocalizations. Many people recognize the importance of active listening. Some people are even able to do it. But what they may not realize is that they're often listening to the wrong frequency – their own.

We want to create *connection*. But our inability to listen to the frequency others are speaking creates the opposite. Many years ago, I was sitting at a kidney-shaped table near the back of a classroom listening to the heartfelt pleas of two parents. They were sharing how their daughter was struggling with anxiety and having massive meltdowns when she got home from school.

As I listened to the parents, there was no doubt I wanted to help. I thought what I was about to say would help, too. So I waited for the appropriate time to share something with them. As soon as the perfect time came, I said, "When we see your daughter at school, she is smiling and happy."

It was the honest truth. But it was not helpful. Because it wasn't the frequency they were on. In fact, it was kind of like me changing the radio station on them without asking.

I'm not saying you shouldn't share important information during meetings. I'm not saying your perspective doesn't matter either. But there is a moral to the story. When you fail to honor and acknowledge the wavelength others are on, the *connection* you seek may not materialize.

> The difference-making work you and your team aspire to do requires communication. But you must be able to listen and share on the frequency others are using.

The Great Mini-Cinnamon Roll Conflict

When people approach an issue with different expectations, it's a lot like trying to communicate on different frequencies. As you read the following story, look for examples of expectations being imbalanced.

Our school recently stopped serving mini-cinnamon rolls for breakfast in our cafeteria. We're looking to add back menu items with fewer artificial sweeteners. But what we failed to account for was the passion and fervor students had for their mini-cinnamon rolls. The change was met with student petitions, mini protests, and a clear call-to-action from our students: "End the ban on mini-cinnamon rolls!" We initially chalked up the energy to kids being kids. But the energy only seemed to intensify.

Several staff members and I eventually found time to meet with the students involved. The day of the meeting, we walked into a classroom ready to present our rationale. We were also excited to offer students the chance to sample future breakfast menu options. But when we arrived, students had a different plan in mind.

As we walked into the room, students started re-arranging tables and setting up. For *their* presentation. They held signs, displayed charts, and recited facts about the sugar content of some of our other breakfast items. They also asked some very good questions.

After listening to what they had to say, we attempted to clarify that mini-cinnamon rolls had not been "banned." Technically, they had been rotated off the menu. But when students asked when the mini-cinnamon rolls would return, we didn't have a plan. As you can imagine, rotating an item off the menu indefinitely feels a lot like a ban. It turns out, students weren't overly excited about the promise of free samples either.

The meeting may have started differently than we expected. But we eventually shifted to a posture of listening—on the frequency students were on. This helped create a more connected experience. Setting aside the mindset and messaging we had planned to share created space for us to connect with what students had to share. Therefore, the 5-Fluency Framework isn't just a tool for you to organize your own thinking—it's designed to help you see and hear what's important to others as well (see figure 4.6).

I'm going to walk you through how to use the framework as a tool to navigate conflict in the next section. But I want to share a quick thought on something I call "expectation management" first.

Anytime two or more people have different expectations, there's a reasonable chance there will be conflict of some kind. The conflict may not involve petitions and posters. But it could involve things that are just as important. Like disappointment, frustration, or a quiet erosion of trust. Having different expectations than another person is not bad.

Figure 4.6: The great mini-cinnamon roll conflict

But you might be operating on different wavelengths and not even realize it.

> The ability to look at an issue and understand how another person is experiencing it is invaluable. It can help you create deeper and lasting *connection* more quickly than all the free samples in the world ever could.

How to Create Connection

Many people have a genuine desire to communicate effectively. To hear and be heard. They want to build positive relationships and make a difference. But they don't always know how. Or they don't know that they don't know how.

I made a promise to you early on, and I intend to keep it. I want you to be able to see (and hear) the small and solvable parts of complex issues, so that you can do the difference-making work you aspire to do. In the Introduction of this book, I compared using the 5-Fluency Framework to having a Heads-up Display (HUD) projected onto the windshield of a vehicle. There are a few different ways to do this.

One way is to practice looking for the fluencies consistently. This is a mental exercise. When you are facing a challenge, try to imagine the framework in front of you. You get to choose which fluencies to access and how to make a difference using them.

The other way is more tangible. Sometimes I will draw a quick shorthand sketch of the framework when I'm in a meeting or when a phone conversation starts to feel complicated (see figure 4.7).

To do this, I'll sketch a quick 2x2 matrix and fill it in with the first letter of each fluency (C-A-M-P). This helps me be able to continue listening to the person talking, without having to think too hard about what the fluencies are.

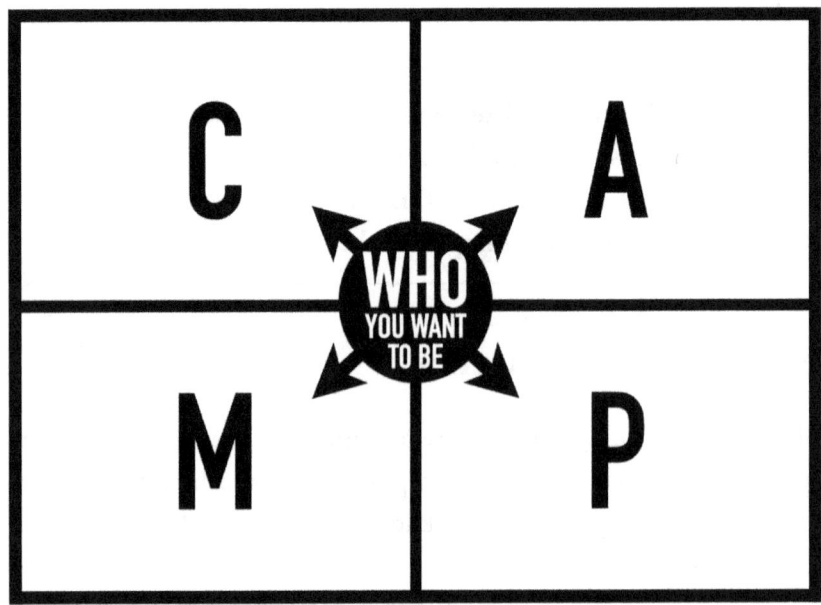

Figure 4.7: Quick shorthand sketch showing the fluencies (CAMP)

After I have completed the shorthand sketch of the framework, I continue to listen. I write down some of the precise words and language the other person is using. But I'm strategic in where I write my notes. I actually add them to the framework space that seems to fit what the person is saying. The goal is to honor their perspective while paying careful attention to what's important to them.

If they tell me something that's important, I may jot it down in the priorities (P) box. If they share their ideas or reveal how they're thinking about the issue, I may jot it down in the mindsets (M) box. I try not to alter their word choice or convert what they're saying to how I would say it—unless they happen to say something offensive.

The shorthand note-taking strategy helps me think about what somebody is saying in the frequency it's being said. This is a lot more effective than changing what I'm hearing to fit my needs or perspective.

> **Communication is a gift. Even when it's hard to hear. The language, questions, and stories people share are a window into how they're experiencing education. If you truly want to create *connection*, try to focus on the essential fluency on which people are communicating.**

Think, Know, and Be (Exercise)

Communication can be tricky. You can't control what people will say, how they'll say it, or whether they'll copy the School Board and superintendent on their emails to you. But learning how to think differently about communication is in your control. It's also a skill.

OVERCOMING EDUCATION EXERCISE
THINK, KNOW, AND BE

This exercise will help you reflect on some of the beliefs and skills you brought to this chapter. But it will also help you reflect on how your thinking may have changed. Before you begin, I'd encourage you to revisit the Quick Response Scenario from the beginning of this chapter. Rereading the perspective or advice you planned to share in that scenario could serve as a good reminder of the beliefs and strengths you started with.

I'd also encourage you to consider that large number I shared at the beginning of this chapter. You may recall, 90% of all parents believe their child is at (or above) grade level. I'm sure there's a joke about everyone believing their child is gifted in this statistic. However, I also wonder if there's an opportunity for us to reflect on *Who we want to be* as educators, communicators, and partners in learning.

1. First, complete this sentence:
   I used to **THINK** *communication was...*

   _____
   _____
   _____.

2. Next, complete this sentence:
   Now I **KNOW** *communication is...*

   _____
   _____.

3. Last, complete this sentence:
   Moving forward, I want to **BE** a person who...

   _____
   _____
   _____.

COMMUNICATION: HOW TO SPEAK THE LANGUAGE OF CONNECTION

The Language of Connection

For all we know, President Jimmy Carter might have actually connected with that audience back in Japan—if only his interpreter had given his joke a chance to land. And Senator John McCain's campaign might have gained more momentum—if only he had been prepared to talk about his priorities differently before that fateful emergency meeting.

Have you ever read a quote and been so convicted by it that you just had to share it?! George Bernard Shaw once said, "The single biggest problem with communication is the illusion that it has taken place." This is not just a problem politicians experience. Most people have experienced misunderstandings, miscommunication, and a failure to create *connection* a time or two.

But at the end of your day, week, or career, you are the single-greatest factor in how you choose to communicate. Making a difference can be done in many different ways. But it almost always requires connection. First on the inside and then with others. But, it's not easy to connect when you're on a different frequency than others. This doesn't mean your frequency is wrong; it just means you or somebody you care about might miss out on an important message.

> Education can be overwhelming. But making a difference doesn't have to be. In Chapter 5, we'll explore some key strategies to help you make a difference on the things that matter most: your priorities! We'll also look at some pitfalls that can cause teams to get stuck.

CHAPTER 5

Priorities: Moving Beyond Common Ground

We're more than halfway through the essential fluencies—that's a big deal! You're learning how the fluencies can help you break complex challenges into smaller parts. And how the fluencies can work together to enhance the impact you and your team make. Which can be helpful when trying to move priorities forward.

In this chapter, I'll share a few strategies to help you and your team make progress on your priorities. Together. No matter how challenging things may seem. By the time this chapter is over, you'll be more aware of some pitfalls that prevent people from making progress. But you'll also be more equipped to do something about it.

The Forest Man

I'm always amazed at the lengths people will go when something is important to them. It's pretty incredible when you stop and think about it. In 1979, a boy named Jadav Payeng stumbled upon a startling scene.[101] As he was walking along the banks of the Brahmaputra River near his family's home, he discovered scores of dead snakes scattered across the sand. With no grass or tree cover for shade, they never stood a chance against the sun.

In the years preceding his discovery, flooding and changes to the flow of the river had decimated the landscape until all that was left was sand. Lots and lots of sand. Jadav feared his community would be overcome as well. So he planted a tree in the sand. But he didn't stop there. He kept planting trees—for more than forty years.

When he first started, people dismissed his efforts as absurd. But today there is an expansive forest in the northeast region of India that begs to differ. What started out as a desolate landscape where snakes go to die has been transformed. It's now a thriving ecosystem that's home to tigers, monkeys, elephants, and many species of birds. And for every tree Jadav planted over the years, the wind spread countless seeds, multiplying his effort over time. Now people around the world affectionately refer to Jadav Payeng as, *The Forest Man from India*.

The time and energy Jadav invested into planting trees* leaves little room for doubt about his commitment to growing a forest. He wanted to make a difference—and that's exactly what he did.

This story demonstrates the extraordinary lengths people will take when something is important to them, similar to the extraordinary effort educators put into making a difference. But as inspiring as Jadav's story might sound, your situation is not the same.

Jadav Payeng Worked Alone

When Jadav Payeng decided to plant his first tree, he didn't get much pushback. Nobody was there to tell him that his tree-planting technique

---

* *Planting one tree in the middle of the sand might sound like a fool's errand. But taking "smalvable" steps adds up over time. With hundreds of thousands of trees, Jadav Payeng's forest is now comparable in size to Martha's Vineyard, a 100 square-mile island located off the coast of Cape Cod.*[101, 102]

PRIORITIES: MOVING BEYOND COMMON GROUND

was incorrect. He was alone. Unless you count a bunch of dead snakes as company.

Education can feel isolating, too. But you are probably not alone. Most of us rely on support from others. Even if the "support" sometimes feels like red tape, unfunded mandates, and other things we wouldn't necessarily choose for ourselves. The fact remains, we are part of a larger educational ecosystem, an ecosystem that can also be hard to change.

There's a reason it might feel more like you're putting out fires than planting trees. The number of responsibilities on your plate is not small. I'm confident you can come up with your own list. But here are a few priorities that might sound familiar:

- **Being responsive to the student mental-health crisis and discipline concerns.** Whether you're teaching in a classroom or supporting the needs of an entire school or system…you already know that the struggles our students experience impact the learning environment profoundly.
- **Keeping pace with technological advances that are transforming many facets of life outside schools.** From artificial intelligence to challenges associated with social media and ubiquitous connectivity…you are at the epicenter of the transformation of society and its impact on learning.
- **Increasing achievement for all students while addressing gaps in opportunity and success.** High-stakes testing and the expectation of accountability continue to be part of our reality. You are responsible for supporting students who may be struggling with trauma, housing and food insecurities, and other complex challenges. But you cannot prioritize achievement for *all* without prioritizing the basic needs, dignity, and inherent worth of *each and every*.

- **Improving culture while navigating budget reductions and staffing shortages.** It's a little on the ironic side. Amidst all these complex challenges is the overriding importance of creating a healthy, safe, and positive culture. Navigating budget cuts while simultaneously creating a culture people want to be part of is not for the faint of heart. Neither is trying to teach or run a school while you're covering a colleague's classroom.

The priorities you're carrying are not the same as Jadav Payeng's. These are not priorities you can carry alone—which creates another challenge.

> People have different levels of readiness when it comes to priorities and new ideas. Therefore, learning how to determine where they're at is a skill. Honing this skill will help you and your team move the work that matters most forward.

Priority Pulse Check (Exercise)

You don't have to carry priorities alone. But in order to carry a shared priority with other people you must communicate. If you're not having meaningful conversations about shared priorities (and progress!) on a regular basis, you might not have shared priorities. You might just have disparate beliefs, isolated actions, or pockets of excellence.

OVERCOMING EDUCATION EXERCISE
PRIORITY PULSE CHECK

PRIORITIES: MOVING BEYOND COMMON GROUND

Now that you have a sense of what this chapter will focus on, I want to invite you to participate in an exercise that will help you notice how often you and your team are talking about your priorities. For this exercise, we're going to do a "pulse check" of sorts.

Try to think about a priority that you and your team share. This exercise is an opportunity to notice how many times you talk about that priority with the people around you over a certain period of time. You could decide to do this for the next hour, day, or several weeks; the period of time that you choose is not the point.

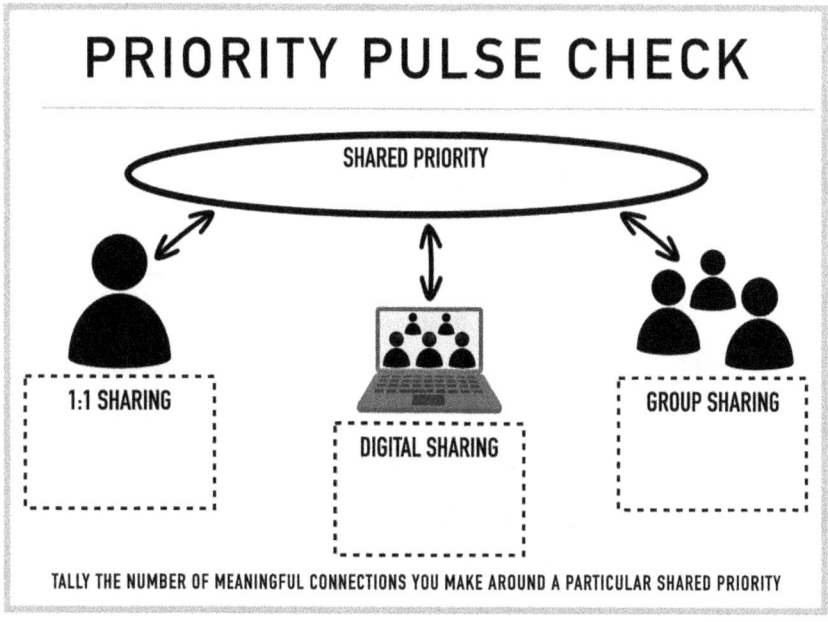

Figure 5.1: Priority pulse check

1. Start by identifying a priority you and your team share. Write that priority in the oval (see figure 5.1).
2. Next, try to notice anytime you mention this priority when communicating with other individuals, groups, or using digital communication (e.g., email, newsletters, and social media).

3. Then, place a tally mark in the box that corresponds with whatever type of sharing you engage in.
4. Finally, take some time to reflect on the data you collect after a period of time. What do you notice? How often does your communication reflect shared priorities and with whom?

The Priority Pulse Check is one way to think about how often you're talking about things that matter most. It also provides you the opportunity to think about the degree to which your tally marks reflect *Who you want to be* when it comes to championing what's important.

To be perfectly candid, there have been times in my career when I wasn't engaging in enough meaningful conversation about shared priorities. I tend to carry priorities internally. I think about them often and try to align my actions with them. However, this can leave a lot to be desired when it comes to creating culture and developing a shared understanding of priorities.

> People carry priorities. But if you're not talking about what matters most, how will anyone know what you're carrying? Or what it looks, sounds, and feels like to carry priorities together?

People, Priorities, and Blockbuster Movies about Shark Attacks

One of my priorities in writing this book is to help you get really good at seeing the five fluencies beneath the surface of your challenges. Learning to look for the fluencies can help you break complex challenges down into more manageable elements, so you can make a difference on the work that matters most to you and your team. But this is less likely to happen when priorities are unclear.

On June 20, 1975, the biggest blockbuster Hollywood had ever seen was released.[103] A half-century after hitting theaters, the energy behind *Jaws* is not fading; the movie has become a cult classic.* The American Film Institute named the Shark from *Jaws* the 18th best villain of all-time.[104] LEGO immortalized the movie in August of 2024 when it released a 1,497 piece set featuring the iconic Orca boat being attacked by a shark. Before we go too far into the deep end of movie nostalgia, I want to share some numbers from the movie that will be important as we move forward.

400

"Jaws" was the first movie ever to be released in more than 400 U.S. theaters. It was also the first movie to gross over $100,000,000.[103]

1 Hour 21 Minutes

One of the draws of "Jaws" was the fear it elicited as people anticipated seeing the massive great white shark. Most people are surprised to learn you don't actually see the shark until 1 hour and 21 minutes into the movie.[103] *You might catch a glimpse of an occasional fin or swirl of water before then. But the shark doesn't appear until well into the movie.*

3%

As the story goes, the mechanical shark had more malfunctions during the filming of "Jaws" than its director, Steven Spielberg, had

---

* The previous footnote in this book used Martha's Vineyard as a size comparison to show just how big Jadav Payeng's forest became. The fictional town in 'Jaws' was shot on location in Martha's Vineyard – off the coast of Cape Cod, Massachusetts. Due to strict land ordinances, the production team was only allowed to build one permanent structure for the set. They chose Quint's shack. All the other structures—like the famous Amity Island billboard—had to be constructed and taken down in the same 24-hour period.[103]

anticipated.[103] *Therefore, Spielberg had to find ways to ominously suggest the menacing creature was present without actually showing it. This led to the shark only appearing for four total minutes—which is only 3% of the movie.*[105]

I share these numbers to provide you an important contrast. When it comes to priorities—don't be like *Jaws*. Make your priorities clear. Talk about the mindsets and ideals that your priorities are connected to more than 3% of the time. Reference *Who you want to be* relative to your priorities early and often.

People need more than assumptions and vague hints to carry the things that matter most forward together. They need to be part of the production team. As a tribute to *Jaws*, I want to invite you to look at the fluencies beneath the surface of the water and how they connect to your priorities (see figure 5.2).

Now would be the perfect time to cue up the ominous *Jaws* theme-song music. Da-dum...... Da-dum...... DA-DUM DA-DUM DA-DUM!

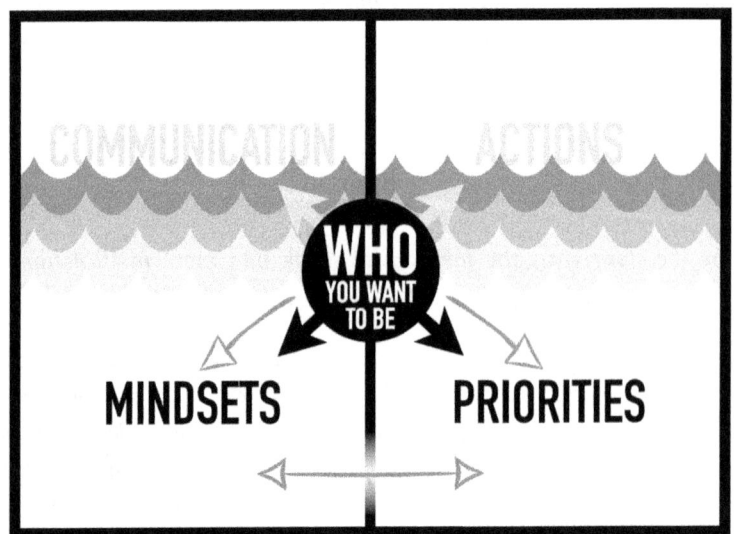

Figure 5.2: A look at the fluencies beneath the surface...

PRIORITIES: MOVING BEYOND COMMON GROUND

The connection between your mindsets, priorities, and *Who you want to be* is crucial. Priorities cannot exist apart from people–at least not very well. So keep this mindset on your radar as we dive deeper into priorities.

Another mindset you will notice as you read this chapter is the importance of carrying priorities together. The idea that collaboration can enhance your priorities is not new. Neither is the concept of finding common ground. However, the concept of common ground is often misunderstood, which is why we're going to go down a bit of a rabbit hole.

The next three sections are dedicated to clearing up a few things about common ground, so that when you and your team are carrying shared priorities you can avoid some common pitfalls.

A Brief History of Common Ground

The history of common ground is a story about survival. It's also a good starting point to understand some of the nuances involved in how we work with others. Our ancestors lived in small bands of 30-50 people.[106] They spent much of their time gathering plants and hunting. Yet, meeting their basic needs was not their only challenge. Survival depended on their ability to quickly distinguish between friends and foes. Failure to tell the difference between the people they were cooperating with and unknown threats came with grave consequences.

Over time, the human brain has become very efficient at categorizing people as friend or foe.[107] But this automated sorting system is far from perfect. Which can create another problem. Your brain is still labeling people as "friends" and "foes." But instead of protecting you from enemy clans or attacking tigers, your brain started shielding you from different ideas and the people who carry them. This makes it challenging to find common ground with anyone who thinks differently than you do.

When our brains label ideas and people as "foes," we can miss out. Other people are an invaluable source of perspective. They can reveal blind spots and elevate ideas. The automated labeling our brains do may have helped our ancestors survive. But it is not making it any easier to work with people who have challenging behaviors and approaches to communication.

The Tyranny of Familiar

People mistake finding common ground with moving forward. We tend to talk about common ground like it's this transformational place. A place where compromise abounds and progress automatically happens. But common ground doesn't always work that way.

Common ground can be the place where your loftiest goals go to die. The psychology behind this is a little bit scary. But if you're aware of it, you can interrupt it. People gravitate to things that are familiar to them, even when superior options exist.[108] Researchers from two separate studies used the familiar topic of baseball to study the conversational tendencies of people. But their decision to use baseball was not arbitrary.[108]

A staggering number of baseball statistics are generated each year. Nowadays, statisticians measure everything from wins and losses to exit velocity and spin rate.* All this data made it easier for researchers to measure the performance of players people chose to talk about in casual conversations.

---

*Spin Rate refers to the rate a ball rotates in the air after a pitcher has thrown it. The higher the rate of spin, the more movement a pitch will have, making the ball harder to hit. In 2016, a pitcher with the New York Mets, Seth Lugo, threw a wicked curveball that was measured at 3,498 rpm. The pitch was the highest-spin curveball that had ever been tracked—more than 1,000 rpm higher than the average Major League curve at the time. The opposing player struck out swinging and the Mets went on to win the game.[109]

PRIORITIES: MOVING BEYOND COMMON GROUND

Participants in the first study were provided a list of several baseball players, along with their statistics for the season. Half the players on the list were well-known names who had just completed mediocre seasons. The other half were lesser-known names who had just had statistically-superior seasons. Can you guess who people chose to talk about? Results from the first study showed that in general conversation, people picked well-known names to talk about. Even though better players existed!

The second study was set-up a little differently.[108] It tracked media mentions of specific baseball players in the top 50 U.S. newspapers for several years. Baseball players who were mentioned more by the media ended up being talked about more frequently in online discussions held by the general public.

This might not surprise you. But here's the thing. There were players with better career statistics as well as players with recent breakout performances who weren't being talked about by the media. Therefore, the general public wasn't talking about them either. They were statistically superior, but less familiar.

I had a startling epiphany when I read these studies. You and I are not immune to the same social-psychological pull that participants in these studies experienced. But instead of talking about familiar baseball players, we might be talking about familiar practices. Even though superior options could exist.

There was another aspect of this study you'll want to know about as you navigate common ground. The general public overwhelmingly settled for talking about familiar baseball players instead of those players who were achieving excellence. But experts talked about the superior statistics and players experiencing success at a higher rate.

Knowing this should give you some confidence as an educator. Because you have expertise within the field of education. But you'll still want to be intentional.

> **Seeking common ground can be a helpful starting place. But it isn't always the needle-mover we make it out to be.**

Beyond Common Ground

I don't want to make finding common ground sound inherently bad. It is not. It can take really good and intentional work to get to common ground with another person. Mostly because people are tricky. And working with people who are not always easy to work with is even trickier.

All of this can make finding common ground feel like a significant accomplishment. This is one reason people tend to confuse finding common ground for something it's not. We may think we've moved to where another person is at—which is true to an extent (see figure 5.3). But by its very definition, common ground is meeting somebody where you're at, too. Therefore, just because you've moved closer to another person's interests, doesn't necessarily mean you've made progress on a priority.

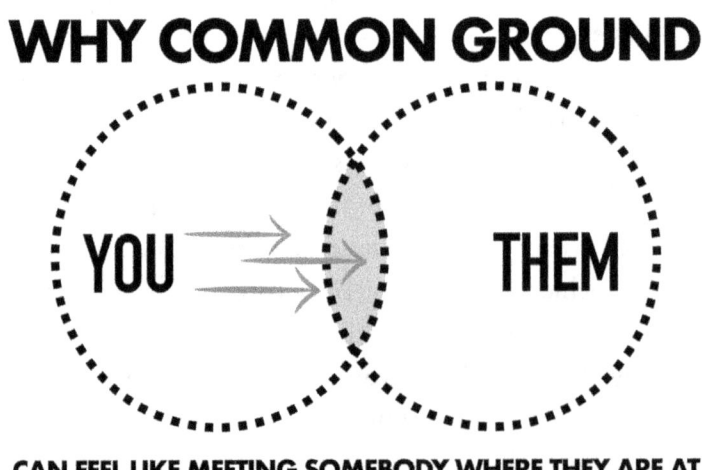

Figure 5.3: Venn diagram showing common ground

PRIORITIES: MOVING BEYOND COMMON GROUND

Meeting others where they are fully at requires a different kind of movement and thinking. It involves a willingness to go beyond where you are currently standing in the hopes of understanding another person's needs, perspective, and Netflix preferences—even if you have a hard time understanding why they want to binge watch certain shows.

At the beginning of this chapter, I shared the mindset that priorities don't exist apart from people. Therefore, trying to push priorities forward without an understanding of where people are at doesn't work very well.

The rest of this chapter is dedicated to helping you get really good at learning where people are actually at. So that you can meet them there. To listen, learn, and co-create priorities that you can carry together.

The Places People Frequent

Ideas need people in order to become priorities. But not just any people. To become priorities, ideas need people with the capacity to carry them forward. However, it's not always easy to know where others are at. Or what their capacity is. Not everyone walks around sharing their deepest motivations and fears. Workplace politics, cultural norms, and bosses who claim to want feedback but struggle to hear it can hinder authentic sharing.

It is helpful to know some of the places people are at when it comes to moving ideas forward just in case they're not announcing their capacity on a public-address system. But before I share these common places, I want to caution you from using them to label the people who visit them.

With this in mind, here's a framework showing some of the places people stand when it comes to moving ideas forward (see figure 5.4). I use the word "ideas" intentionally. Simply calling something a priority doesn't mean others see it the same way.

WHERE DO YOU STAND
WHEN IT COMES TO MOVING IDEAS FORWARD?

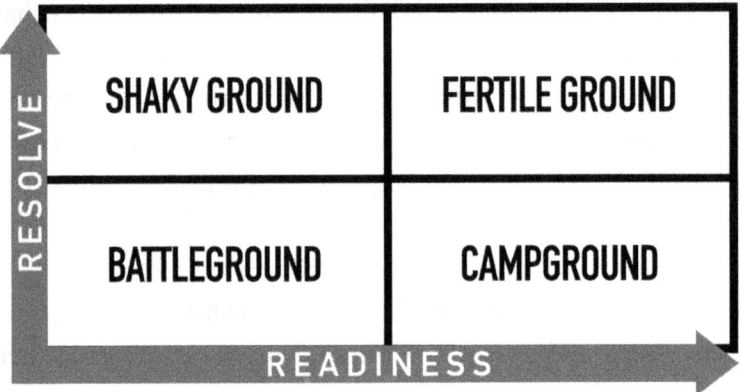

Figure 5.4: Where do you stand – framework

The quadrants within the framework are shaped by two things: a person's *readiness* and their *resolve*. Readiness involves the skills and capacity somebody has to carry a specific idea forward. Readiness is fluid. It can be increased through conversation, professional learning, or by simply including a person in the development or decision-making process.

Resolve involves a person's commitment and motivation to carry a specific idea forward. Just because a person appears to have a lower-level of commitment towards one idea doesn't mean their resolve will remain lower for other ideas. Therefore, resolve is also fluid. Here's a short summary of each quadrant:

Battleground

When you're visiting the Battleground quadrant, you have very little readiness or resolve to move a particular idea forward. In fact, you're more likely to resist or fight the idea—in a cognitive sense.

PRIORITIES: MOVING BEYOND COMMON GROUND

People in this quadrant may be feeling overwhelmed with other commitments. Or they may not be feeling overwhelmed. It could be that systemic issues like a loss of trust, frequent miscommunications, or false starts from a department chair or central office are impacting their resolve.

From a strengths-based standpoint, people who are in the Battleground quadrant are not uncommitted or unwilling to champion ideas. Sometimes they're already committed to a different or competing idea. Instead of writing them off as a lost cause, try showing up curious.

Campground

When you're visiting the Campground quadrant, you have high readiness and low resolve to move an idea forward. It's a bit of a juxtaposition. But just because you have the capacity, skills, and bandwidth to pack up your camping gear doesn't mean you're motivated to do so.

From a strengths-based standpoint, people who are standing in the Campground quadrant could be doing so for all the right reasons. Perhaps they are setting new boundaries for their relationships and work. Or maybe they are more motivated to invest their time and energy into better ideas. Instead of trying to get their buy-in, your energy may be better spent seeking to understand what it is that they're motivated by.

Shaky Ground

When you're standing in the Shaky Ground quadrant, you have a high level of resolve to move an idea forward. But your readiness level is low. This can happen when you believe in an idea, but lack some of the skills or bandwidth needed to move the idea forward. This can result in a lack of follow-through or mistakes during execution.

From a strengths-based standpoint, being on Shaky Ground is nothing to be ashamed of. It can show you are open to new learning. You might just need additional time, support, or training. Instead of assuming a person who says, "Yes" to an idea has everything they need, look and listen for ways to move the idea forward together.

Fertile Ground

When you're standing in the Fertile Ground quadrant, your readiness and resolve to move an idea forward are high. The conditions for your best work and thinking are largely in place.

It's easier to meet ideas from the Fertile Ground quadrant when you've been included in the process. Being included transforms the soil. Effective communication and reasonable levels of support also help create higher levels of readiness and resolve.

From a strengths-based perspective, Fertile Ground is a place where meaningful ideas have a chance to move forward. But it is not a promise they will (or even should) move forward. Fertile Ground is not a place where everyone says, "Yes." Productive discourse can take good ideas and make them better. Instead of treating Fertile Ground like a destination, try to cultivate the soil—no matter what ground you and your team happen to be standing on.

Most people spend time in different quadrants throughout the day depending on the specific ideas they're interacting with. It's also possible a person could be in multiple places simultaneously. This is especially true when you're working through complex issues.

The Backfire Effect

Moving ideas forward should not be a seamless process. If you don't encounter speed bumps, you're probably missing important voices and perspectives. However, it's also possible you and your team will experience unproductive or hurtful pushback from time to time. Moments like this are not fun. But understanding some of the neuroscience behind why people struggle with ideas is helpful. When somebody pushes back really hard against an idea, it could be they're protecting something deeply important to them. So they fight back.

This is called the "Backfire Effect."[110] Neuroscientists discovered that when people are presented with information that challenges their core beliefs and political leanings, it triggers the same part of the brain that would be activated if they were attacked by a shark (see figure 5.5). If you need a more realistic example, imagine seeing a spider on your desk instead of a shark.

Examples of beliefs that might trigger the Backfire Effect include how a parent views their child, how a co-worker views their teaching practices, and almost anything connected to politics. One of the most interesting parts of the Backfire Effect is that the brain doesn't just fight back. It actually fortifies whatever core belief it's trying to protect.

The good news is this psychological response is not something that happens all the time. Your brain doesn't need to go into protector mode if the idea or information you receive doesn't conflict with deeply entrenched beliefs.[111]

Figure 5.5: The Backfire Effect

For example, if I told you starfish* do not have brains, you might be surprised. But there's a very good chance you'd accept this information without wanting to fight me as long as I provide sufficient evidence. This is because the information can co-exist along with other information that is more central to your beliefs and worldview.[111]

Understanding the psychology involved when working with people and ideas is important. Having a general awareness and empathy for where they might be meeting ideas is helpful, too. However, being strategic with how you approach conversations about ideas really makes a difference.

---

* It's true. Starfish do not have brains.[112] The 15,000 tube feet covering their bodies act autonomously when responding to the environment. The tube feet synchronize their movements to travel through the ocean. Engineers have been studying the phenomenon for years with the goal of applying the science to robotics.

Three Strategies in One

I made a promise to you very early in this book. I told you I was going to help you see the small and solvable parts of complex challenges. The framework and fluencies are an essential part of this. However, you can also break each individual fluency down into smaller and more strategic parts. This is particularly true of your priorities.

Here's a strategy that can boost a person's readiness and bolster their resolve like no other. It's not fancy. But it does involve three parts. I haven't decided what to call the strategy yet. But I'm leaning towards calling it the "Trifecta of Pure Gold." Because that's how solid it is. Here are its three parts:

- Purpose (Doing work that's meaningful)
- Progress (Celebrating small steps)
- People (Doing the work with others)

When your ideas and priorities tap into all three parts, it will be hard to stop them from moving forward. Research on organizational culture found people were 373% more likely to have a strong sense of purpose when these three things were accounted for.[113] But that's not all.

They were 747% more likely to be highly engaged at work when purpose, progress, and a *connection* to each other were established. **If you and your team want to take an idea and transform it into a priority you can all carry, anchor your work in purpose, celebrate incremental progress, and carry it together.**

In another study involving 238 people from seven different companies, researchers analyzed 12,000 daily survey responses.[114] They wanted to understand what is happening when employees are at peak creative output.

Data showed that on days when people made progress, their motivation levels increased, which means their resolve increased as well. This is great because a big part of meeting ideas on fertile ground requires resolve. But this isn't the only thing that changed in people who made some form of progress.

The study also found that the people who made progress started to perceive their challenges differently. So much so, they experienced fewer setbacks and had more "good days." Participants who had "bad days" did not recognize making any progress, and their data was almost the mirror opposite of those who had a more positive inner-work life.

Purpose. Progress. People...

Making progress on work that is meaningful matters.[114] But when the progress is informed by the voices of the people closest to the work, it elevates everything. That's because people who have a voice in what gets prioritized are eight times more likely to carry feelings of trust.[113] This is true of classroom culture, organizational culture, and the culture of your car on family road trips. **Decisions made *with* people are greater than decisions made *to* people.**

If you want to increase your commitment, motivation, and resolve, look for ways to make incremental progress and see what happens. Take time to notice, understand, and celebrate progress. Together.

Hope for Tomorrow

There is always hope. But sometimes people have a harder time finding it. Therefore, it's helpful to learn how hope can be generated. Even when things are really hard.

The gruesome conflict between Israelis and Palestinians has been going on since the late 19th century.[115] I won't pretend to understand all the complexities involved. But I know it has been brutal. Finding common ground has not always felt possible in the Middle East. But there have been some breakthroughs over the years.

PRIORITIES: MOVING BEYOND COMMON GROUND

In 1978, President Jimmy Carter mediated peace talks between Israeli Prime Minister Menachem Begin and Egyptian President Anwar Sadat. The talks were held at Camp David, a presidential retreat in Catoctin Mountain Park, Maryland.

For twelve days, the two sides were locked in a tense stalemate. So much so, the two leaders didn't want to be in the same room together. The only common ground they could find was a deep distrust and animosity for one another. However, on the twelfth day something shifted.

President Carter asked the leaders about the future they wanted for their grandchildren. Within hours of describing that future, the groundwork for an agreement was in place—and Sadat and Begin went on to win the 1978 Nobel Peace Prize.[116]

This story is not a one-off. You and I can tap into the same psychology when we are stuck in unproductive places. Or when we're trying to work with others who might be stuck. But don't just take my word for it.

Olga Maria Klimecki-Lenz is a Swiss neuroscientist and mediator. She studies how the brain controls feelings that help people get along. Her work with people who are experiencing conflict and hostile conditions can help us understand the science of getting unstuck. She suggests that emotions like hope hold the power of moving towards peace.[115]

In related research, participants were asked to think about their future for one minute. A control group was asked to think about random animals. After these interventions, each group played a game with other people. The participants who had reflected on the future were found to be much more helpful than the people who thought about animals.[115]

When people think about the future—even if it's unrelated to a conflict or priority—it can positively influence their situation. This is similar to the approach President Carter used at Camp David. **People say hope is not a strategy. But I think they might be wrong.**

I don't know the innovative work, complex issues, and inspiring change you and your team are engaged in. I don't know what frustration, hurt, or lunchroom supervision duties your co-workers are carrying either. But I do know that thinking about the future you want to create makes a difference. So does inviting others to do the same.

Education can be overwhelming. But making a difference doesn't have to be. There is always hope. And thinking about the future can create it.

Validating Doubt and Disbelief

You might have noticed the open-ended nature of this chapter. In other words, I did not tell you what your priorities should be.

You could be thinking:
"This feels really open to interpretation..."

It's true. The fluencies are not prescriptive. They reflect the essence of making a difference. But they do not tell you what to prioritize. Or how you should prioritize it. That work is adaptive and requires your expertise and discernment.

The 5-Fluency Framework was designed to pair with the strengths and priorities your team has. Not to replace them. With that said, I hope I've shared some insights and research to help you be more fluent in understanding your priorities and connecting with others on priorities that are shared.

Moving Forward

Jadav Payeng didn't have to worry about finding common ground. He worked alone. So all the ground was his. As an educator, you will encounter people who don't always agree with you. Some of these people will provide you with the gift of pushback and additional perspective. Others will be downright difficult to work with. But this doesn't mean you can't make a difference together.

Think about the future you want to co-create. Keep leaning into feedback and trying to understand where people are standing. Seek out opportunities to co-create ideas. Work together to carry the ideas that are meaningful forward and watch as they emerge into powerful priorities. But be careful not to treat your priorities like the shark from Jaws—make time to talk about what matters with your team.

> **The next step on our journey is to turn your priorities into actions. Chapter 6 will help you get started. I'll see you there!**

CHAPTER 6

Actions: Subtle Shifts Can Change Everything

Can you taste it? You've honed your skills and sharpened your ability to focus on four of the five transformational fluencies. You're SOOO close to being able to see the small and solvable parts of larger problems. Yet, something strange can happen with the final fluency.

When it comes to taking action, our brains can revert to that of a teenager trying to focus on homework right after texting their crush. It's not easy. Therefore, I'm going to share a quick story to help you and your team *not* lose your minds when deciding what actions to take. The story also reveals the theme for this entire chapter.

The Power of Subtle Shifts

It's the summer of 2015, and I am sitting on a blue bench inside a *flight center* just north of Chicago. Waiting for my turn to fly. Technically speaking, I'm sitting on a bench hoping I won't severely embarrass myself or die.

I'm usually in a hotel room the day before speaking—obsessing over my notes and the message people might need to hear. But a few other people who are also speaking at the conference invited me to this blue bench. This is my first time indoor skydiving. And wearing a red onesie. Eventually, somebody wearing a blue onesie with a patch that says "Flight Instructor" approaches me. I can't hear him over the roar of the massive wind tunnel towering in front of me. But for some strange reason, I get up and follow him inside the deathtrap.

We're immediately met by a 120 m.p.h. blast of air.* It is crashing up at us through a grated floor. The force is so intense I'm literally having trouble moving. And breathing.

Suddenly, my goal of not embarrassing myself or dying feels like it's in jeopardy. My instructor braces me and somehow tips me into a floating horizontal position. For the next thirty seconds, I flail around the tube, like Santa diving headfirst into first base. In full disclosure, there's a lot more clunking into glass than floating happening.

However, another thing happens. I do not get sucked up into the giant metal fan blades at the top of the tunnel. The fact that I don't die makes me feel a little less embarrassed, too. I find my way back to my blue bench after my turn ends. As I'm staring back into the wind tunnel I just conquered, I notice my instructor is still inside. Flying solo. And it is nothing short of spectacular.

He reminds me of a real-live superhero defying gravity. As I lose myself in the moment, I can't help but notice how effortless he's making this look. One moment he's flying up near the fan and the next he's gliding around the center of the tunnel. Which makes me really jealous.

---

* *In actual skydiving—the kind where a person jumps out of a perfectly good airplane— it takes 3-5 seconds to reach a terminal velocity of 120 miles per hour.*[117] *I did not have 3-5 seconds to work my way up to that speed. I hit terminal velocity the second I cowered into the wind tunnel. (The cowering was mostly due to the giant metal fan blades spinning overhead that appear like they will severely injure me if I accidentally float up too high.)*

ACTIONS: SUBTLE SHIFTS CAN CHANGE EVERYTHING

Because I want to fly like that. So now I'm thinking, *How is it possible he looks like Superman in the same space I struggled to breathe?*

I look closer. Then I see it. As my instructor cups his hands, he jettisons upward. He makes other subtle movements, too. When he arches his back, he stops gliding and hovers ominously in the middle of the wind tunnel. Now, I'm having this epiphany...

Education can feel like a 120 mile-per-hour blast to your brain, heart, and ego some days. It's hard. It's humbling. But the chance to take action on things that make a real difference is incredible.

> Education is not the same as skydiving. The stakes are higher. But there are subtle shifts in education, too. Therefore, understanding the power of subtle shifts can mean the difference between clunking around the bottom of a giant wind tunnel or flying. That's what this chapter is all about!

Less is Smart

We do a lot of adding in education. Many of the things we add are good, too. But adding more, and more, and more good things is not always better.* Yet, our actions, school improvement plans, and state standards seem to suggest otherwise.

I remember my first principal position. I had just attended a training on writing SMART goals. I learned that great principals set specific and timely goals. And I wanted to be a great principal. So I set seven specific and timely goals.

---

* *The Law of Diminishing Return tells us more can actually be worse. I'm not sure why I remember this. But my college economics professor explained it like this: If you were given one can of Mountain Dew to drink you might really enjoy it. However, if you were given an unlimited supply of Mountain Dew you might not appreciate it as much after consuming six or seven cans. In a metaphorical sense, there's a lot of Mountain Dew being served in education.*

To this day, I don't remember what all the goals were. But I do remember how good it felt to write them. It felt good to post them on our school's website, too—which is where those seven goals sat collecting digital dust for much of the school year.

I still think about my mistake. Instead of working as a team to co-create 1-3 goals we could truly focus on, I buried our opportunity in big words and good things. Which made it really difficult for anyone to understand what really mattered. I know I'm not alone in trying to add "just one more good thing" to my plate. Or the plates of others. But as I've said before, **you can only fill a plate so full before it breaks the person carrying it.**

This is why the radical act of reducing is so important. Resisting the urge to add more can help you and your team take action. We do not need...

More work.
   More words.
      More good things.
         More on our plate.
            More in our schedule.

We need to practice the intentional act of reduction. I was recently working with a team who embraced this subtle shift with passion. It was one of the coolest experiences I've been part of. However, it didn't start out that way.

We were wanting to write a district goal pertaining to Multi-Tiered Systems of Support (MTSS). To be clear, we were only writing one goal (not seven!). But by the time everyone had embedded their pet words into the goal, it was way too clunky.

The goal we had created sounded really smart. But any goal you need to reread three times to understand is not smart. So we started stripping it down. Way down. Until it reflected the essence of *Who we*

ACTIONS: SUBTLE SHIFTS CAN CHANGE EVERYTHING

wanted to be relative to our MTSS work. The final result was a goal that was clear, memorable, and dare I say–exciting. It all started when we challenged ourselves to reduce.

We did include several short action items underneath the goal. This was our way of ensuring the specific actions we wanted to take were clear. Without bogging down the goal itself.

> **Sometimes you need to *do less* in order to accomplish *more*. Because *more* is not necessarily smarter. This subtle shift can inspire action.**

The One Thing Most People Aren't

A lot of people can do the right thing once or twice. The same applies to hard things. And difference-making things. But it takes effort and intention to do these things with consistency.

I shared a story about a college football player struggling to get playing time earlier in this book. In 1995, Tom Brady was the 7th-string quarterback at Michigan.[16] At that time, his odds of becoming Michigan's starting quarterback were about the same as Michigan's groundskeeper. Yet, Brady went on to become one of the greatest quarterbacks the NFL has ever seen.

I revealed some insights into how he overcame the odds in the Introduction. But Brady shared something during his 2024 Hall of Fame induction speech that you'll want to hear.[118] And I'm paraphrasing here...

"You don't have to be special to be successful at anything. You just have to be what most people aren't. Consistent, determined, and willing to work for it–no shortcuts."[118]

I'm not a New England Patriots fan. But I appreciate good advice as much as the next person. What Tom is saying is that doing the right, brave, or important thing once can help. But doing these things consistently can change everything. The same applies to taking small and solvable actions.

Making progress on meaningful work requires consistency. Make a habit of showing up on purpose and for a purpose. You can fool yourself into believing doing something once and doing it consistently are similar. But the results are anything but.

Habit Stacking (Exercise)

We want the actions we're taking to make a difference. But in order for this to happen we need to ensure they stick. Many people think it takes 21 days to form a habit. But this might be more of a myth than anything else.

In the 1960's, a plastic surgeon noticed it took patients approximately three weeks to get used to seeing themselves after surgery.[119] This observation was published in a book around that time—with no formal research being conducted. Ever since then, the 21-day rule has been cited as the magic number for forming habits.

More recent research shows habits are formed fluidly—between 18 to 254 days. With repetition being the biggest factor.[120] However, repetition isn't the only way to make new actions stick. You can help your brain form habits through something called habit stacking.[121]

Dr. Krysti Vo says the brain is wired to create efficiencies.[121] We've explored some of these efficiencies over the course of our journey together. This is how things like breathing, brushing your teeth, and accidentally putting the cereal in the fridge (and milk in the cupboard!) happen. Our brains love patterns. Therefore, if you want a brain-friendly way to build new habits, don't start from scratch. Stack new actions onto well-established habits.

I used habit stacking years ago when I wanted to become a more effective literacy leader. I just didn't know it was called habit stacking at the time. I had already established the habit of using video and social media to communicate. So I used my pre-existing passion for technology and stacked literacy on top.

I started by integrating booktalks into some of the podcasting and social media projects I was already engaged with. That led to me connecting online with authors and literacy leaders. Then, I started embracing literacy leadership in more and more of my work. I even went on to write a book for leaders who want to create stronger reading communities in their schools.

To this day, I'm actively researching, sharing keynote messages, and facilitating workshops to help educators push literacy conversations and practices forward. It's hard for me to fathom that everything started by the simple decision to stack reading onto work we were consistently doing with technology and innovation.

OVERCOMING EDUCATION EXERCISE
THE ART OF HABIT STACKING

This exercise is an opportunity to think about an action you might want to do more regularly. Experts suggest adding smaller habits to your routines.[121] Like adding a few minutes of stretching before you brush your teeth.

1. First, brainstorm actions and behaviors that you might like to do more consistently. Use the Habit Stacking Template to list your ideas (see figure 6.1).
2. Next, think about some of the core habits you already have. (I provided some examples in the lower-right corner of the template.) Choose one core habit or well-established routine and write it in the blank box.

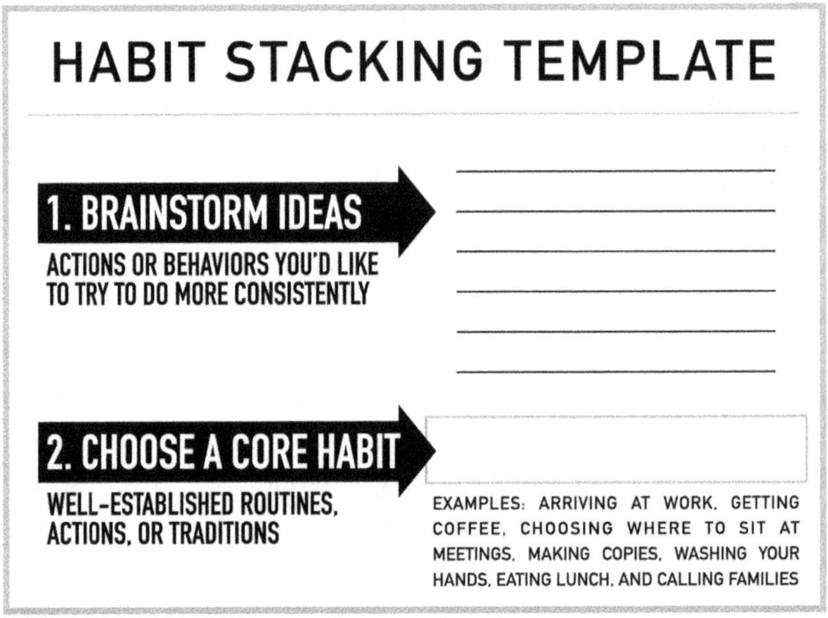

HABIT STACKING TEMPLATE

1. BRAINSTORM IDEAS
ACTIONS OR BEHAVIORS YOU'D LIKE TO TRY TO DO MORE CONSISTENTLY

2. CHOOSE A CORE HABIT
WELL-ESTABLISHED ROUTINES, ACTIONS, OR TRADITIONS

EXAMPLES: ARRIVING AT WORK, GETTING COFFEE, CHOOSING WHERE TO SIT AT MEETINGS, MAKING COPIES, WASHING YOUR HANDS, EATING LUNCH, AND CALLING FAMILIES

Figure 6.1: Habit stacking template

3. Then, reread the list of ideas you brainstormed in step 1. Select (or circle) one that you will "stack" onto your core habit.
4. After that, take action! But be consistent. Whenever you do your core habit, practice the new action you stacked on top, too.

Validating Doubt and Disbelief

There's a chance you might not need to hear this. But I'm feeling compelled to give you a mid-chapter pep talk. As you get closer to the end of the book, it's possible all kinds of doubt and disbelief will surface. Especially while you're reading a chapter focused on taking action.

You might be thinking:
"I want to take action, but I don't know where to start…"

ACTIONS: SUBTLE SHIFTS CAN CHANGE EVERYTHING

If you're unsure of where to start, I'd suggest accessing the super-fluency: *Who you want to be*. Think about *Who you want to be* in relation to whatever challenge you're facing. Then, think about the smallest possible action you can take to be that person. After that, take action! Whatever you do, don't discount the small steps you take that flow from *Who you want to be*.

Or you could be thinking…
"I want to take action, but the problem is the system (and fighting the system is exhausting!)…"

You are not wrong. Many of our challenges are systemic in nature. Yet, a significant portion of this book has focused on identifying small and solvable things you can control. Therefore, we haven't spent a lot of time addressing how to lean into larger issues that feel outside our control. This has been intentional. However, before this chapter is over, I'll share a framework to help you address complex challenges on multiple levels—including those that involve systems.

Seeing the Connection

Deciding *Who you want to be* is a choice any of us can make. However, taking actions that reflect your ideal self when everyone else is telling you not to is hard.

Jamie Kern Lima is on a mission to help people understand their inherent worth. And if actions speak louder than words, she's absolutely nailing it. But her actions are not arbitrary. They are on purpose. Kern Lima is an entrepreneur, champion of women, and one of the founders of IT Cosmetics.[122] IT cosmetics started in Kern Lima's living room in 2008. Eight years later, she sold the company to L'Oréal for $1.2 billion.[123] She's continued to lead IT, becoming the first female CEO of any L'Oréal brand in its more than hundred-year history.

It would probably be easier for me to list the few television shows that have *not* featured Jamie Kern Lima. Yet, for all the success she's achieved, one thing stands out more than others. She has prioritized living out her mission with authenticity. Kern Lima has a skin condition called rosacea.[122] It's a hereditary condition that causes rough, red skin blotches to appear on her face. Even though she's in the television and skin-care business, she regularly removes her make-up to ensure people see the real her.

While this might sound like a small thing, her livelihood depends on the perceived effectiveness of her skin-care products. Therefore, her decisions have been revolutionary within an industry that's not necessarily known for truth in advertising. In a make-or-break moment, Kern Lima went against the advice of industry insiders.[122] They told her removing her make-up on air would be a mistake. They also said skincare products sell by showing consumers "unattainable beauty." But she valued being real over portraying perfection.

She decided to market her products using models who represented real women of all ages, body shapes, and with different skin challenges. More than a billion dollars later, her actions have inspired a loyal following.

Did you notice how Jamie Kern Lima's actions reflected her priorities? She not only knew *Who she wanted to be*, she aligned her actions with her priorities and purpose.

I have a feeling you want to be the kind of leader whose actions reflect your core beliefs. You wouldn't have made it this far on our journey if this wasn't the case. Therefore, the subtle shift I'm about to highlight might sound more like common sense to you than anything else.

Think about the connection between your priorities and actions (see figure 6.2). Even as you're taking action. Name that connection. Take time to help others see it as well. Notice when the connection is not as strong as you want it to be. And work with your team to strengthen and align it.

ACTIONS: SUBTLE SHIFTS CAN CHANGE EVERYTHING

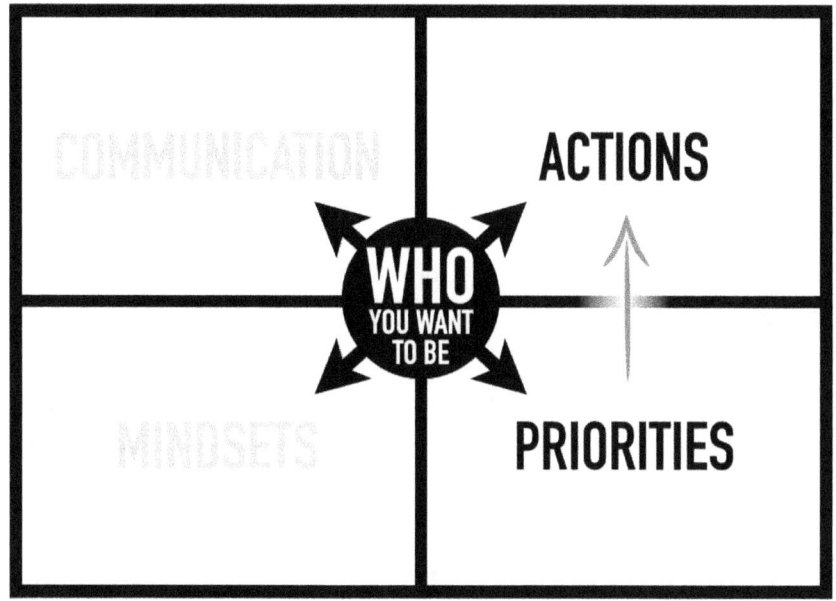

Figure 6.2: The connection between priorities and actions

> The distinction between *deciding* a thing and *doing* a thing may seem small. But crossing the chasm between deciding and doing is everything. Therefore, translating your purpose and priorities into authentic actions is a small and mighty thing.

The Stockdale Paradox

I'll get to the Stockdale Paradox in a moment. But I'm going to front-load it with some basic psychology so your brain can maximize the power of the paradox.

Actions do not exist in a vacuum. They flow from our priorities and patterns of thought. Therefore, understanding how the brain functions can help you bring more intention to what you actually say and do. Our brains are wired to simplify the world around us.[124] I've mentioned some of the psychology behind this throughout the book. Another way we simplify things is by reducing complex issues into false dilemmas, or false dichotomies.

I see this done in politics quite often. For example, when people pit economic growth against environmental protection, they're creating a false dichotomy. I believe it is possible to have a nuanced conversation about economic growth *and* environmental protection. Yet, many people frame these issues as either-or options.

You're not immune to the same psychological tendency as an educator. If you listen for *either-or* arguments you'll hear them quite often. Presenting a complex topic with limited options is an either-or fallacy.[124] It's also very similar to creating a false dichotomy. An example of this would be trying to boil education down to being about relationships *or* results. In reality, education can be about both.

Admiral Jim Stockdale spent seven years as a prisoner of war in Vietnam.[125] He saw many comrades die during this time. When asked how he survived, Stockdale shared that he always had faith. But he also accepted the brutal reality of his situation. The same article shared a story Stockdale told about his fellow prisoners. He said, "The optimists…they were the ones who said, 'We're going to be out by Christmas.' And Christmas would come…and go." The cycle repeated and they eventually died of broken hearts.

Stockdale contrasted their optimism with the approach he used to survive.[125] He never lost faith he would get out. However, he also accepted he might not get rescued anytime soon. This became known as the Stockdale Paradox. Having faith *and* confronting reality.

I know of no other way to say this—and I also recognize the analogy is flawed. There are things about education that are very hard. Seeing students struggle. Seeing colleagues struggle. And struggling yourself. But we can name the hard things *and* keep the faith.

ACTIONS: SUBTLE SHIFTS CAN CHANGE EVERYTHING

> It's such a subtle shift. But developing the capacity to be optimistic *and* realistic can help you frame issues in a more nuanced and inclusive manner. Which can lead to your team taking actions that are capable of overcoming hard and complex things.

Creating Constellations

Educators have a lot of responsibilities. I recognize "a lot" is not an exact number. But I'm pretty sure it's accurate. A nationally representative survey conducted by the EdWeek Research Center reported teachers work about 54 hours a week.[126] However, just under half this time–46%–is spent teaching. The rest of their time is spent on things like grading, providing feedback on student work, planning and preparation, general administrative work, non-student interactions, collaborating with colleagues, communicating with families, doing committee work, professional learning, attending after-school events, and more.[126] Did I mention teachers do a lot?!

When I work with teams and organizations, I often compare the number of responsibilities in education to stars in the sky. There's a reason I make this comparison. But let me share a really, really, really big number with you first.

200 billion trillion

Astronomers estimate there are 200 billion trillion (a.k.a. 200 sextillion) stars* in the universe.[127] This is a number so big that I had to spell it out because I wasn't confident I could fit all the zeros across this page!

---

* *To calculate the total number of stars in the universe, astronomers take the number of stars in a typical galaxy and multiply that number by the number of galaxies in the universe. The Milky Way has around 100 billion stars – and there are two trillion galaxies.[127] Therefore, they estimate we have around 200 sextillion stars in the universe.*

88

However, from the 200 sextillion stars in the sky, the International Astronomical Union only recognizes 88 constellations.[128] *That's not exactly a small number, but it's significantly less than 200 billion trillion.*

So here's why I compare the responsibilities of educators to stars. You cannot focus on 200 sextillion things. But it is possible to focus on a constellation of things. When we think about our priorities in terms of being part of a constellation, we increase the clarity of our intentions, which supports people taking meaningful action on shared priorities.

Taking time to create a shared understanding of the priorities shining brightest—and how those priorities connect to other initiatives—is important. It's also a strategy you and your team could use or adapt. I created an example of a constellation our team has used (see figure 6.3).

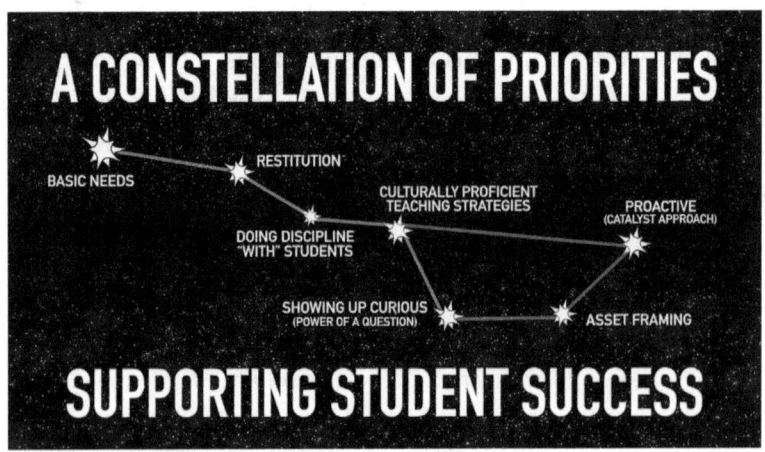

Figure 6.3: Constellation of priorities (example)

You can see some of the initiatives and work our team is engaged with in the example. Seven priorities probably seems like a lot.

ACTIONS: SUBTLE SHIFTS CAN CHANGE EVERYTHING

However, these are not all new initiatives. The constellation represents some work we've been engaged with for several years—as well as a small number of emerging priorities. Including a combination of well-established and newer priorities provides people solid footing from which to take action on emerging work.

People tend to appreciate when their past work and learning is acknowledged as well. And seeing how the initiatives they're investing in connect to the broader vision. But more than that, they value having a voice in the process. This strategy can help create a space where conversations about removing things from people's plates (or solar systems) can also happen.

If stars aren't your thing, you could use sticky notes or create a bulleted list. The theme is not the point. Identifying priorities and organizing them into mental models that are actionable and sustainable is what matters. Connecting your team's stars is a subtle thing. But the process can strengthen culture and build collective efficacy.

> **Leadership is helping others see the things that matter most, like a constellation of priorities, so they can move forward with the confidence that their actions are an important part of the collective effort.**

Becoming "O.P." and "Broken"

It seems like kids are inventing new words all the time. Or assigning new meaning to old words. I often just shake my head and smile when I hear my teenagers doing this with their friends. Mostly because I'm confused. But I recently made a connection between something my son said and a powerful concept in education.

My son and I started playing the Pokemon card game together several years ago. We battle each other using decks of cards that contain creatures with unique abilities. Over the years, we have each developed some pretty formidable decks.

However, my son recently informed me that some of the cards we have been using were "broken." A card is deemed broken when it affects the balance of a game more than it should. These decisions are usually made by the gaming community, not my son. All of this to say, I'm no longer allowed to use my Sneasel (cartoon weasel) card. Evidently, it's overpowered and too good! Or as my son would say, "It's O.P. and broken."

Solving complex challenges is different from playing Pokemon. But there is a card you can play that is so positively influential it could be considered overpowered and broken—and it's called *collective efficacy*.

Collective efficacy refers to the shared belief that you and your team can make a difference in students' learning more than the factors that are outside your control.[129] Basically, the research shows when a group believes they can make a difference—and when they organize their actions around this belief—they actually do make a difference. A big one!

If I were designing a playing card showing how powerful collective efficacy is, here are the stats I'd include on the back of the card:

3x

Collective efficacy is three times more predictive of a student's achievement than their socio-economic status.[130] Therefore, you and your team have more control over what students can learn than where they live or what the income of their family is.

2x

Collective efficacy impacts learning twice as much as a student's past achievement.[131] Therefore, every school year is an opportunity to unlock new and hidden potential.

ACTIONS: SUBTLE SHIFTS CAN CHANGE EVERYTHING

#1

Collective efficacy is a big deal. It has the largest effect size of all the factors included in Hattie's meta-analysis.[130] The effect size of teachers' collective efficacy is 1.34. To provide some context without getting out over my skis, the average effect size was 0.40 in the 2,100+ meta-analyses. Therefore, how you and your team think about your students is the number one difference-maker when it comes to their success.[130]

Identifying the small and specific shifts that lead to such "O.P." results is important. You can start by believing the work you do to help all students connect, learn, and grow is more powerful than a student's address or past achievement level. Another way to practice collective efficacy is to talk about the influence you have and the difference you can make. Then, organize your systems and actions around that belief. Because it's true.

> **Collective efficacy is a belief in action. And small actions make a big difference. When you and your team organize your actions around the belief all students can learn–they do!**

The Almost Invisible Triangle

I promised you that I'd help you see the small and solvable parts hidden inside complex challenges, which is why we've focused on looking for five essential fluencies within the work you are doing. However, I want to introduce an additional framework to help you see your challenges differently.

I call it the *almost invisible triangle* and it is made of three levels: Self, Team, and Systems (see figure 6.4). Complex challenges almost always involve more than one level. However, our locus of control tends to be greatest closer to the base of the triangle. Which is why the space around "Self" is comparatively larger than the other two levels. But this doesn't mean you can't influence the upper levels. In fact, you are part of those levels, too. (That's why the lines between the levels are dotted instead of solid.)

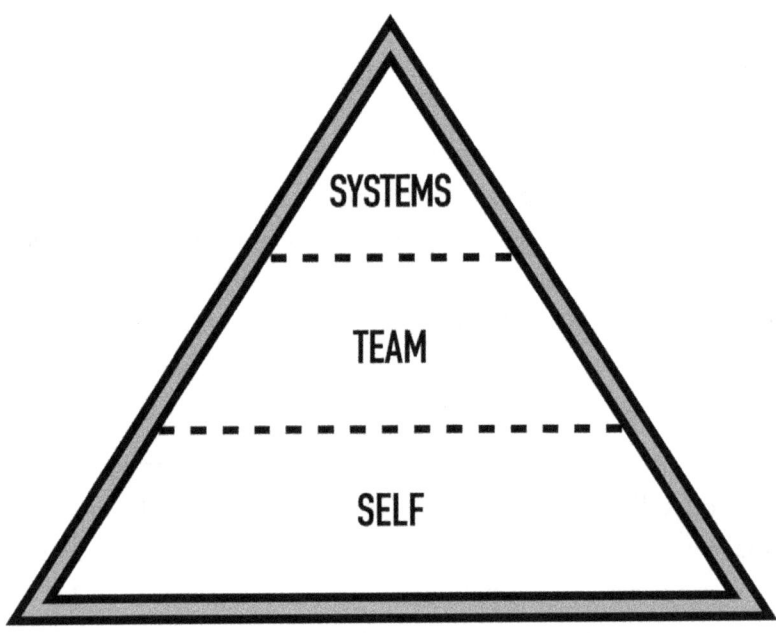

Figure 6.4: The almost invisible triangle

Next time you and your team are talking about how to take action or respond to an issue, try noticing what level of the triangle you're spending the most time talking about. Great leaders consider every level. But the best leaders understand the importance of leading themselves first. So that's where we'll start…

Self: This is the level at which you have the most influence and control. Therefore, it's often possible to make an immediate difference in this space.

ACTIONS: SUBTLE SHIFTS CAN CHANGE EVERYTHING

Team: I use the term "Team" loosely. Your team could be you and a group of students. Or it could be a department, school, or school district. How you apply this term relates to your position and context.

Systems: The term "Systems" could apply to the policies and culture you're operating in. However, an aspect of systems-thinking many people miss are systems that haven't been created yet. Therefore, it is possible for individuals and teams to create systems and influence larger-scale change without needing major support from the entire system.

An example of this might be a team that co-creates a system to collect data on how and when student support is being accessed throughout the school. The system the team creates could be used to maximize existing resources in order to be more proactive with support staff. This "systems change" doesn't necessarily require resources from the larger system to implement.

Sometimes people think "Systems" refers to some distant entity that is untouchable, unchangeable, and generally unhelpful. But when they're working properly, systems provide structure and consistency to help us meet our goals. And it's possible for teams and individuals to create them.

It can be tempting to point your finger at one of the levels in the triangle above you—especially when things are not going well. Focusing on what another level *should* be doing is an option. However, it's an option that might decrease your ability to overcome.

To be clear, I am not suggesting teams and systems should be given a free pass when it comes to constructive criticism. However, I am going to keep it real. You do *not* want the actions or inactions of a leader or system to have absolute control over your wellness and how you view your work. It might not feel fair that we sometimes need to co-create solutions at the "Self" or "Team" levels. Yet, the time you and your team invest in looking for solutions within your control says a lot about *Who you want to be*. It also makes a big difference. But don't just take my word for it.

Social Proof

Small shifts can change everything. However, people shouldn't have to guess which subtle shifts to make.

Lippert is a global manufacturing company known for engineering components for recreational vehicles, watercraft, and prefabricated homes.[132] They are known for having a strong culture and global sales numbers with lots of zeros behind them. But ten years ago, they were known for something different.

They were losing people faster than they could keep them. Their culture was not good and their annual employee turnover was 130%.[133] Their CEO made a series of small shifts to address the problem. One of which was bringing on Kim Lisiak Fraleigh as the Director of Leadership Development.

She shared how Lippert started holding regular listening sessions during which people leaned into questions like, "What's going well?" and "Where could we do better?" But that's not all. They worked together to co-create core values that reflected *Who they wanted to be*. Leaders took the feedback and made additional investments in break rooms, parking lots, air quality, and more. And the results speak volumes. The company cut their turnover rate by more than 100%.[133] They continue to focus on building a better work environment for the more than 12,000 employees they serve.

But there are a couple of other shifts Kim Lisiak Fraleigh made— you might recognize at least one of them. Lippert empowers all team members to see themselves as leaders. People with influence. They do

ACTIONS: SUBTLE SHIFTS CAN CHANGE EVERYTHING

this by coaching all employees on three leadership competencies: Leading self, Leading team, and Leading the business.[133]

Lisiak Fraleigh's philosophy resonates with me. Without even realizing it, our team's approach to tackling complex challenges has mirrored her leadership development methods. While I can't guarantee your revenue will match Lippert's, I do know that focusing on the three levels of the triangle can have a profound impact.

Many of us are painfully aware of systemic issues and factors outside our control. However, increasing our ability to flexibly shift between Self, Team, and Systems when trying to take action is a subtle thing that can make a big difference.

> **Not all leaders lead from formal leadership roles. Everyone can make a difference. We can create opportunities for everyone to lead by learning to see different levels within complex challenges.**

Your Green Light

Education can be overwhelming. But making a difference doesn't have to be. Especially when you know small actions can change everything. Like when skydivers cup their hands; this subtle movement creates more surface area to catch the air. Which creates extra lift.

I'll be the first to admit you should not take skydiving advice from somebody who could barely fly in a wind tunnel. But I am going to leave you with one additional skydiving anecdote. Because you and your team will want it before you jump to action.

There's a three-light system in most jump planes known as a traffic light. When the light is red the plane is not in the correct location and the pilot is not ready for you to jump. But just because the light turns green doesn't mean you should jump either.[134]

Skydivers are trained to use their eyes to locate their designated landing zones before they jump out of an airplane—this is called spotting.[134] Knowing your final destination is something every skydiver needs to think about before they jump.

Before you give yourself the green light to take action, be sure you and your team have practiced spotting. Look for the connection between *Who you want to be* and what you're about to do. Talk about this connection. As well as the other subtle shifts you want to make.

> **Some of the struggles you and your team are navigating are so complex that it's tempting to think your actions need to be complex, too. But complex solutions can make it harder to take action. Therefore, identifying the subtle shifts you and your team *can* make is an important skill. It's also something you can practice today. The final chapter will help you do just that!**

CHAPTER 7

Finishing Strong

Y ou are absolutely crushing it. There's no doubt in my mind you want to make a difference. You made it to the final official chapter, and you're on the verge of being able to say (and believe): **"Leadership can be overwhelming. But making a difference doesn't have to be."**

Therefore, we're going to make darn sure we finish strong. In the remaining pages, I'm going to do everything in my power to help you be able to answer three questions with a hard, "YES!"

Here are the questions you'll be able to come back to when you're finished reading, so you can answer for yourself. (Until then, I included my best guess for how you'll respond).

1.) Did this chapter affirm the important work I'm already doing *and* inspire me to take action? (YES!)
2.) Did this chapter deliver on the promise of helping me see the small and solvable parts hidden inside every complex challenge? (HECK YEAH!!)
3.) Did this chapter provide me with practical strategies so I can start applying this to my work immediately? (YOU BETTER BELIEVE IT–YES, YES, YES!!!)

Now, let's finish strong so you and your team can make the difference you aspire to make.

The Return of Blue Scuti

In the first chapter of our journey together, I shared a story about a teenager who goes by the screen name, "Blue Scuti." He made national news when he did something no other human had ever done. He was able to crash the classic arcade puzzle game, Tetris. But not only that, he beat the game with a level of efficiency that Artificial Intelligence (AI) hasn't been able to replicate.[22]

In a media interview after the accomplishment, Blue Scuti said, "*If you try hard enough and set your mind to something…you will get it.*" This is inspiring advice. But it may not apply to the complex challenges you're facing. Therefore, you are the reason this book exists.

You're shaping the future. There's no single playbook, algorithm, or computer code that could guide you through the unpredictable challenges you face each day. You and your team are navigating societal, cultural, and technology-driven changes that are happening so fast they would make Blue Scuti blush. And if you're anything like the educators I get to work with, you're doing it with humility, grace, and fewer meltdowns than you're entitled to.

Thank you for being committed to learning and growing, too. You've already taken several important steps to get to this point in the book. This says a lot about *Who you want to be*–and you already know I think that's a very big deal.

Thank you for enriching my learning along the way. Whether it's been through conversations at conferences, connecting via social media, or simply sharing space as you read this book. I appreciate your *humanity* and *connection*. (This may sound crazy, but I'm getting a little emotional as I write this.)

Please let me know if there's anything I can do to support you and your team moving forward. There's a contact link on my website (BradGustafson.com). I've created a study guide that includes discussion questions as well as some scenario-based challenges. The guide is free (and fun!).

> This work we get to do can feel overwhelming at times. But you're doing it. You're dreaming big on behalf of your students. There have probably been more than a few times when you've even prioritized the needs of students over your own needs or the needs of your family. That's hard. I want to genuinely acknowledge everything you are pouring into this profession. But I also want to help.

The Art of Reduction

There are many things competing for your time and attention. Some of these things are important and others are even more important. But everything is NOT an emergency.

Rick Rubin is considered one of the most influential record producers ever.[135] His work is legendary and it transcends genre. But for all his creativity and genius, Rubin has never tried to add to a song in order to improve it. It's been just the opposite.

The first album he produced was with LL Cool J in 1985. But instead of writing, "Produced by Rick Rubin," the album says, "Reduced by Rick Rubin."[136] When asked about this, Rubin shared his goal is to help artists get down to the purest form of their music.[136] He likened finding the essence of a song to building a strong foundation from which to build. This made me think of you.

You can practice reducing challenges down to their essential nature. Just as a chemist knows water is formed by bonding two hydrogen atoms with one oxygen atom, you know the fluencies are actively working together anytime you build relationships, trust, or make progress on an ambitious goal (see figure 7.1). The five essential fluencies are the DNA of making a difference.

Figure 7.1: How the five essential fluencies work together

Of course, seeing the small and solvable parts of complex challenges is important. But being able to take your next step and make progress is also important.

I've shared at least one question for each of the five essential fluencies below. The questions are intended to help you continue the journey we're on after you and your team finish this book. Feel free to make the questions your own—or work together to create better questions.

Who do you want to be?
- Does what I'm about to say or do reflect *Who I want to be*?[137]

Mindsets
- What mindsets might be important for me to think about and access in this situation?
- Are there any mindsets present that might need to be paused or interrupted?

Communication
- What frequency is [First Name] using to try and communicate with me?
- What would meaningful communication look like, sound like, and feel like in this moment?

Priorities
- What problem are we trying to solve?
- What are the priorities we want to drive this communication or action?

Actions
- What is the smallest step we could take right now to make meaningful progress?
- How will we celebrate progress and the actions we're taking?

Picking an essential question and practicing it on a regular basis is a strategy you can implement immediately. The more consistently you and your team ask certain questions, the more you build culture.

Sympathetic Resonance

When you practice the art of reduction you might start to notice that progress feels more attainable. Something starts to change in the culture, too. Other people are more likely to resonate with what's being focused on. Making a difference is contagious.

As a subtle nod to Rick Rubin, I want to share another example that relates to music. There's a little-known phenomenon that occurs between stringed instruments (e.g., pianos and guitars). When the conditions are right, one stringed instrument can cause another to vibrate.[138] But the phenomenon extends beyond stringed instruments. It can be observed in tuning forks, too (see figure 7.2).

When one tuning fork is struck it can cause other tuning forks to vibrate at their natural frequency.[139] Basically, the vibration coming from the original tuning fork activates the others. This is called "Sympathetic Resonance."

SYMPATHETIC RESONANCE

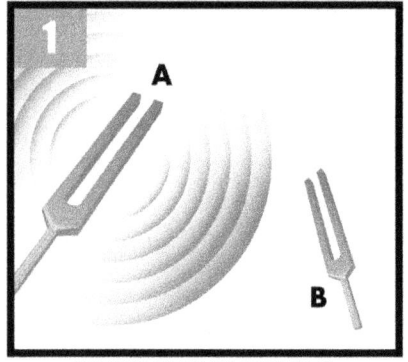
TUNING FORK "A" VIBRATES

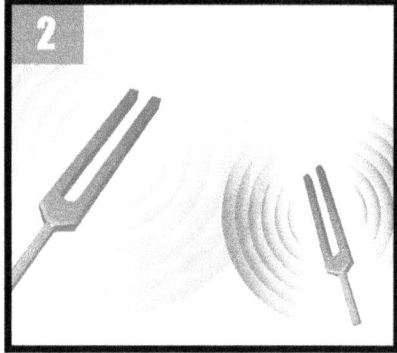
THEREFORE, "B" BEGINS TO VIBRATE

Figure 7.2: Sympathetic resonance between tuning forks

The same principle applies to making a difference. The sympathetic resonance of *Who you want to be* can cause others to be more intentional with *Who they want to be*. The sympathetic resonance of your communication can be a catalyst for others being more intentional with the words and language they use to talk about this work. Transformational leaders are a lot like tuning forks. But the resonating goes both ways.

There's a quote from Anthony Muhammad that inspires me to be a better person and leader everytime I read it (EVERYTIME!). He says, "Your courage gives me courage." These words make me think of the difference-making work you and your team aspire to do.

Your actions inspire my actions...
　The words you choose influence the words I choose...
　　How you treat all students shows me *Who I want to be*...

Deciding *Who you want to be* is not hard. But being that person on a consistent basis is. Especially when things start to feel overwhelming. A simple strategy I've used to help with this is to keep small tuning forks* near my desk. They are a subtle reminder that what we say and do resonates with others—whether we want it to or not. Therefore, it's important to let *Who you want to be* inspire your words and actions.

> **Never tire of trying to show up as *Who you want to be*. The small things you do as your authentic and ideal self will get repeated. Whether you realize it or not.**

The Candy Cane

I shared a concept I call, "The Candy Cane" midway through the book. I didn't make too big a deal about it then. In fact, it was buried near the bottom of Chapter 3 in a section about poisoned pawns in chess.

---

* *You could skip buying tuning forks and simply reference figure 7.2 for daily inspiration. But then you'd miss the fun of being able to use the real tuning forks in teachable moments with students. The tuning forks I found were fairly inexpensive and came with wooden bases (a.k.a. resonance boxes). The boxes allow me to demonstrate sympathetic resonance similar to the countless sound-experiment videos available online.*

But the candy cane remains one of the most easy-to-implement and effective strategies I use with teams.

You may recall, the name of the strategy comes from the shape your arm makes when you extend it towards another person and curl your pointer finger back towards yourself. When you do this your arm and pointer finger resemble one large candy-cane shape (see figure 7.3).

Figure 7.3: Blaming vs. candy caning

I use the candy cane to remind myself of *Who I want to be* in meetings. But I also use it in challenging situations or when mistakes have been made. Regardless of what others perceive my role to be in a conflict or mishap, there's usually something I could have done differently. Or an aspect of an issue I can own in an authentic way. So I practice candy caning by taking responsibility for whatever I can control. Which could be anything from thinking differently to leading with more intention in the future.

Some might say it's unfair to ask educators to point the finger at themselves when the district should be accountable for its decisions. But using the candy cane has never absolved anyone else from taking their rightful share of responsibility. If anything, I've noticed it creates a culture in which others are even more willing to own their role in challenges. Besides that, most of us are part of "the district."

If you're interested in candy caning instead of blaming, here's a strategy you could put into practice right away. Pay attention when you and your team are leaning into a challenge, struggling to identify your next steps, or when somebody accidentally pulls the fire alarm. If it's appropriate, consider the following steps…

Candy Caning
1. Think about *Who you want to be* in a humble and authentic manner. Consider sharing this aloud if it's genuine and helpful.
2. Acknowledge your role in the challenge. (This is usually where the physical act of candy caning occurs.) If the situation warrants, you might focus on the next steps you'll take to help move forward in a positive manner.
3. Try to move forward by giving yourself and those around you grace. Be intentional with aligning your thoughts, words, and next steps with *Who you want to be*.

Candy caning is not about making a big production or looking backwards. It's about practicing empowered thinking and resisting the urge to shame or blame others.

> Your ability to humbly point to yourself—in any situation—is not something that should be taken lightly. It might be one of the hardest things you learn to do. (And I'll still respect you if you're not ready or interested in doing it.) But it can forge a powerful mindset and help create a culture of collective efficacy.

The Enduring Authority of Small

It might be my affinity for sci-fi. But there are so many connections between space exploration and the opportunity we have as educators.

It's hard for me to resist "going to the well" one more time—especially, since this example demonstrates the authority that small and intentional steps can carry.

The Starlink Satellite Constellation launched by SpaceX is a high-tech reminder that small steps make a difference. SpaceX isn't building a massive constellation all at once. They're creating a mega constellation one small satellite at a time.[140] Each Starlink satellite weighs less than 2,000 pounds at launch. And with every satellite they add to the sky, they move closer to the goal of providing low-cost internet, education, and health services to underserved people everywhere.

But here's the thing. Just because you take smaller steps doesn't mean you'll be immune to pushback—nor do you want to be. Feedback can reveal blind spots and perspectives we might not have considered. In the case of SpaceX, some scientists have shared their concern over the light pollution being created by the 6,000+ Starlink satellites in low orbit.[140] This seems like something important to think about.

Here's a practical strategy to help you access the authority of small while also tapping into the power of pushback. The strategy builds on a basic practice many people already follow. Seeking feedback before implementing an idea, initiative, or trying to change your school mascot is always a good idea. But here's a small iteration that's helped me more times than I can remember. Try collecting feedback that's aligned with one of the five essential fluencies:

1. *Who you want to be*
2. Mindsets
3. Communication
4. Priorities
5. Actions

This strategy can help you break your idea down into small and solvable (a.k.a. smalvable) parts, with each part holding the potential for incremental improvement. Here's an example of this strategy that focuses on communication. Oftentimes, the communication frequency that others meet new ideas on is different than our own. Paying attention to their words, tone, and any worries they share can help you improve how you talk about an idea or change in the future.

Try asking for feedback about an idea from a colleague. Just like you normally would. But try to hear every question and concern your colleague shares about the idea, no matter how small. Even if changes to the idea itself are not needed, the questions and concerns your colleague shares can help you communicate the idea to others more effectively in the future.

> Small doesn't equal unimportant. Small is progress.
> Pushback doesn't equal unkind. Pushback is perspective.

Micromanaging vs. Making Micro-Differences

Micromanaging *people* creates macro problems. But the ability to micromanage your *challenges* is different. It involves staying under control while searching for the smallest parts of larger problems. This is how you make micro-differences. And micro-differences add up.

Over the course of this book, we've explored how you can use the 5-Fluency Framework to manage smaller aspects of complex challenges. But I introduced another framework in Chapter 6. That framework was called, "The Almost Invisible Triangle." You might recall the triangle represents three different levels you could consider when approaching larger challenges.

One thing I didn't mention is how the triangle can also be used in conjunction with the 5-Fluency Framework. Applying the triangle to the individual fluencies is a practical strategy you and your team can try today. But before you do, I should clarify one thing. You do not have to apply the triangle to all the fluencies every time you want to make a difference. It's OK to pick one fluency (see figure 7.4). For the following example, you'll see how the triangle was applied to *priorities*.

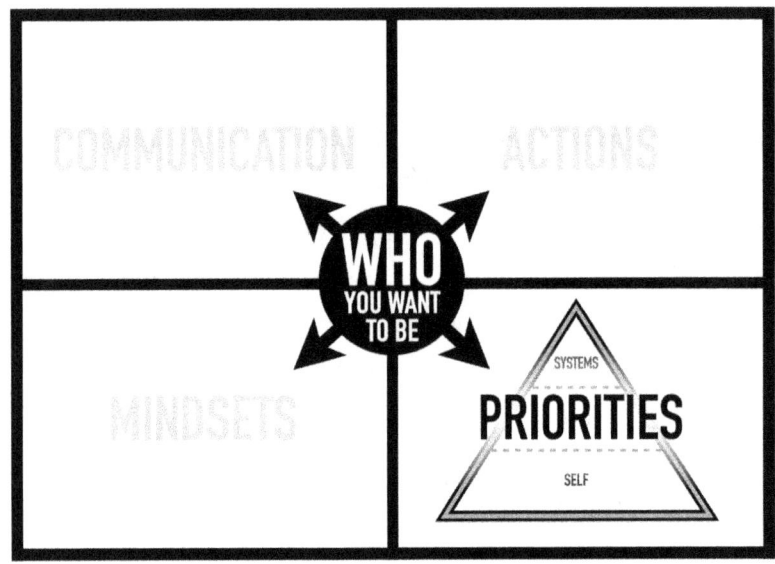

Figure 7.4: The almost invisible triangle in action

Several years ago, our team set out to strengthen the culture of literacy in our school. It was an ambitious goal. Yet, we didn't exactly know how to get started. The framework and *"Priorities"* fluency didn't formally exist at that time. Yet, you can see how some of our initial steps connected to them on different levels.

Self: A priority for me was sharing book recommendations. I was familiar with research on reading motivation from my time serving on Scholastic's Principal Advisory Board. I also knew I could begin sharing booktalks right away. Therefore, this was a small thing I started doing consistently.

Team: Our team worked together to co-create a vision for literacy. It contains two distinct priorities: We want to help all students learn *how* to read and *want* to read. Teams developed goals and action plans aligned with these two priorities. The action plans teams developed included tangible practices to support reading motivation and achievement.

Systems: Several staff members had adopted the practice of sharing their reading lives with students. They were displaying signs in the hallway advertising class read-alouds and books they were currently reading. However, most of this work was being done in pockets throughout our school. There were no systems supporting teachers with the practice.

That changed when members of our school leadership team suggested we make the practice a schoolwide approach. The team unanimously agreed. We co-created some basic structures to support a more clear and consistent implementation. I'm not talking about anything fancy either. We basically gave everyone access to a few signs and templates. We also made sure the approach aligned with our school's shared priority and vision for literacy. Over the years, students have also joined us in the practice.

These examples highlight how we activated priorities at all three levels of the triangle. However, there may be times when your locus of control is limited to only one or two levels of the triangle. It's OK to start small by using a single fluency and only one level of the triangle.

Validating Doubt and Disbelief

We've kept a fairly tight focus on the five essential fluencies throughout this book—with the exception of a few stories involving political gaffes, space travel, and indoor skydiving. However, it's possible you would've liked me to further emphasize something else that's extremely important.

You might be wondering:
"What about building positive relationships and students?!"

I touched upon this earlier in the book when I introduced the framework and fluencies. However, it's such an important question that we will revisit it now. The fluencies in the framework are the essence of what it takes to make a difference in lots of important things.

As I shared in Chapter 2, leaders who prioritize relationships *and* results are seen as significantly more effective than those who focus on just one of these things. Therefore, these are things that should probably be considered when you and your team talk about your priorities and *Who you want to be*.

But building relationships and supporting students are incredibly complex things. Therefore, just saying, "Relationships matter" or expecting somebody to show up and "relationship" isn't necessarily helpful. However, focusing on the building blocks of healthy relationships and trust is. That's where a focus on the fluencies comes in.

This book is a deeper dive into the essential fluencies that can help you and your team create genuine connection. With yourselves and others. The fluencies can help you grow trust and rally together around the work that matters most—whatever you determine that work to be.

Be Confident—You Can Do This!

The fluencies are one way you can focus on the things that matter most when facing complex challenges. Be confident knowing you have access to these essential elements anytime.

Don't forget, trying to focus on "all the things" is very similar to not focusing on anything. Both approaches make the things that matter most less clear. Therefore, be confident in your ability to discern what matters most in the moment. (Hint: One or more of the fluencies is almost always involved.)

And regardless of what anyone says, not all leaders lead from formal leadership roles. You have insights and understanding that can make a difference in almost any situation. The concepts you and your team have engaged with throughout this book assure me of this. Remind yourself of *Who you want to be* when things are really hard. While you're at it, never forget how powerful this super-fluency is. It can help you make a difference on small things. And small things can change everything.

As our journey on these pages comes to a close, don't forget to give yourself grace. (Don't forget to go back and answer those three questions at the beginning of this chapter for yourself, too.) This work we get to do is not easy. But you can do it!

As educators, we know we make a difference. And the overwhelming majority of people outside education know it, too. Based on the BIG number below, it might be easier to catch a unicorn than to track down somebody who doesn't appreciate the importance of what you do each and every day.

98%

In a world that can feel very divided at times, this is a number worth celebrating. 98% of people believe a good teacher can change the trajectory of a student's life.[11] You know you make a difference; other people know it, too.

I wrote this book to help you and your team make the difference you aspire to make. However, many educators will come to it wishing, wanting, and subconsciously searching for bigger solutions. Mostly because we've got some pretty important (and big) things we're working on.

However, we've been conditioned to believe that dreaming big—and overcoming big challenges—requires bigger steps. But you know this simply isn't true.

> **You know education can be overwhelming at times.**
> **But you also know making a difference doesn't have to be.**
> **My genuine hope for you is that you live this truth**
> **with humble confidence moving forward.**

Acknowledgment

Writing this Acknowledgment has me feeling similar to how I felt going into a staff meeting I held years and years ago. I wanted to apologize for a mistake I had made. But when I walked into the meeting I wasn't sure if I should sit down and share, stand up, or just crawl under a table.

That's kind of how I'm feeling right now. But not because I'm apologizing. I'm actually excited to acknowledge something. However, I'm not entirely sure if this is a sit down and write, stand up and share, or crawl-under-my-laptop-until-I-figure-it-out moment. So, I'll begin by giving you a few final numbers—while I'm still sitting down.

146

The approximate number of times the word "mindset" (or mindsets) appears in this book. I'll let you draw your own inferences. But I think 146 is a lot.

97

The approximate number of times the word "leader" (or leadership) appears in this book. The word "educator" appears around 63 times. This shows our effort to use the terms interchangeably was relatively successful.

1

The exact number of times the word "Jesus" appears in this book (until now). This number is about to increase. But I want to explain why first...

There's a good chance I've invested more time into the book you're holding than almost any other project or endeavor I've ever been part of. That's how important I think the work you're doing is. However, coming out of the pandemic I needed to pause writing this book. Because I was really struggling.

The residual stress from the pandemic–combined with trying to meet the complex needs of students–almost knocked me out of the profession I love. I was trying to help everyone else at school and I wasn't doing a very good job of helping myself. Or being emotionally present with my family.

As you can probably imagine, writing a book about overcoming challenges while struggling to overcome some of those same challenges myself would have taken the word "disingenuous" to a whole new level. So I stepped away to focus on the small things at work that I could control. (Because focusing on the things I *couldn't* control wasn't working very well for me.) Our team has tried to do the same. And it's made a HUGE difference.

Yet, focusing on small and solvable aspects of larger challenges wasn't the only thing that helped me overcome them. (I'm going to stand up now.) It was Jesus. It is Jesus. It's always been Jesus. And this is what I wanted to acknowledge. God has been so faithful to me. Time and time again, He's demonstrated how He can be leaned on when we don't have the strength or answers. I believe this to my core. But that's not all I believe.

ACKNOWLEDGMENT

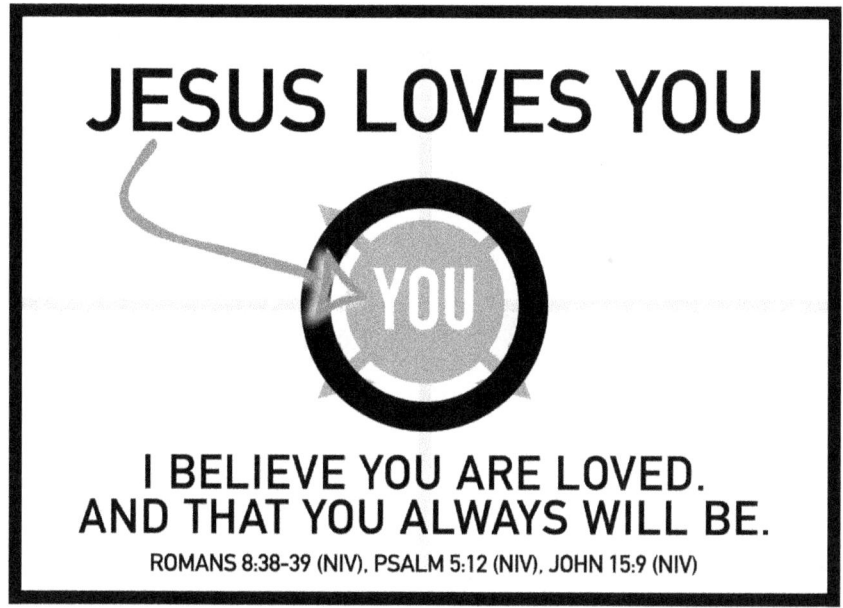

Figure A: I believe you are loved

I believe Jesus is love. I believe Jesus has us wrapped in His love—whether we recognize it or not (see figure A). I also believe we are called to love others.

In Chapter 4, we explored the concept of connecting your communication internally and how important it is to align your communication with your actions, mindsets, and *Who you want to be*—which is what this Acknowledgment is all about. (It means a lot that you stuck around to read it—thank you!)

I'm going to sit back down again. Please reach out if there's anything I can do to help you and your team moving forward. In the meantime, I'll continue to share resources to support your work on my website (bradgustafson.com).

With gratitude and more respect than I could ever hope to convey,

Brad

Notes

Introduction

1. Konstantinovsky, M. (2023, June 9). *You Already Use Heuristics Every Day. Here's What They Are.* HowStuffWorks. https://science.howstuffworks.com/life/inside-the-mind/human-brain/heuristics.htm
2. Shukla, A. (2021, August 14). *Why We Justify Big Events With Big Causes: Balancing causes with effects is an error.* Cognition Today. https://cognition-today.com/why-we-justify-big-events-with-big-causes-proportionality-bias/#google_vignette
3. Kemper, S., Pekel, K., Evenson, A., Seabrook, R., Fynewever, N., & Zhao, Q. (2024). Report of findings from the second biennial Minnesota principals survey. Center for Applied Research and Educational Improvement, College of Education and Human Development, University of Minnesota.
4. Betz, E. (2020, November 30). *If Rome wasn't built in a day, how long did it take?* Discover Magazine. https://www.discovermagazine.com/planet-earth/if-rome-wasnt-built-in-a-day-how-long-did-it-take
5. https://www.rand.org/content/dam/rand/pubs/research_reports/RRA900/RRA956-14/RAND_RRA956-14.pdf
6. Modan, N. (2023, July 12). Superintendents report stress levels double that of other working adults. *K-12 Dive.* https://www.k12dive.com/news/school-superintendents-stress-double/686582/
7. Walker, T. (n.d.). *Alarming number of educators may soon leave the profession | NEA.* https://www.nea.org/advocating-for-change/new-from-nea/survey-alarming-number-educators-may-soon-leave-profession#:~:text=A%20staggering%2055%20percent%20of,its%20members%20released%20on%20Tuesday.

8. Blad, E. (2023, July 19). Could principal apprenticeships expand the pipeline of school leaders? *Education Week*. https://www.edweek.org/leadership/could-principal-apprenticeships-expand-the-pipeline-of-school-leaders/2023/07#:~:text=About%20half%20of%20school%20leaders,a%20career%20change%20or%20retirement.
9. *School leaders, it's time for a Well-Being Self-Assessment*. (2022, November 30). ASCD. https://www.ascd.org/blogs/school-leaders-its-time-for-a-well-being-self-assessment#
10. Diliberti, M. K., Schwartz, H. L., & RAND Corporation. (2023). Educator Turnover Has Markedly Increased, but Districts Have Taken Actions to Boost Teacher Ranks: Selected Findings from the Sixth American School District Panel Survey. In *RAND Corporation Research Report*.
11. Tornio, S. (2021, April 1). *12 Powerful statistics that prove why teachers matter*. We Are Teachers. https://www.weareteachers.com/teacher-impact-statistics/
12. *Address at Rice University on the nation's space effort*. (n.d.). John F. Kennedy Presidential Library and Museum. https://www.jfklibrary.org/learn/about-jfk/historic-speeches/address-at-rice-university-on-the-nations-space-effort
13. Taylor, R. (2023, November 23). *JFK "We choose to go to the Moon" Speech | Transcripts*. Rev. https://www.rev.com/blog/transcripts/john-f-kennedy-jfk-moon-speech-transcript-we-choose-to-go-to-the-moon
14. Pontin, J. (2020, April 2). Why we can't solve big problems. *MIT Technology Review*. https://www.technologyreview.com/2012/10/24/254875/why-we-cant-solve-big-problems/
15. Pickman, B. (2021, February 8). How many Super Bowls has Tom Brady won? *Sports Illustrated*. https://www.si.com/nfl/2021/02/07/how-many-super-bowls-tom-brady-won
16. Wickersham, S. (2021). *It's better to be feared: The New England Patriots and the World They Made*. National Geographic Books.
17. Mohdin, A. (2020, November 19). Gladys West: the hidden figure who helped invent GPS. *The Guardian*. https://www.theguardian.com/society/2020/nov/19/gladys-west-the-hidden-figure-who-helped-invent-gps
18. Pickle, K. (2021, November 24). *Gladys West*. National Center for Women &Amp; Information Technology. https://ncwit.org/profile/gladys-west/
19. Redaktion. (2023, September 21). *ETH Zürich: Kate Maggetti knackt den Weltrekord*. AutoSprintCH. https://www.autosprint.ch/en/aktuell/eth-zuerich-kate-maggetti-knackt-den-weltrekord/

NOTES

20. *Making the case for in-wheel motors.* (2021, July 29). https://www.sae.org/news/2021/07/making-the-case-for-in-wheel-motors
21. *X.com.* (n.d.). X (Formerly Twitter). https://twitter.com/spencerideas/status/1760811870402089057?s=46

Chapter 1

22. Tyson, M. (2024, January 3). Tetris was finally beaten after 34 years, *Tom's Hardware.* https://www.tomshardware.com/video-games/retro-gaming/tetris-was-finally-beaten-after-34-years-game-kill-screen-pops-up-at-level-157-hypertapping-and-rolling-were-key-techniques#:~:text=In%20brief%2C%20the%20killscreen%20happens,how%20the%20prior%20action%20unfolds.
23. PBS NewsHour. (2024, January 4). *WATCH: 13-year-old is first gamer ever to beat Tetris* [Video]. YouTube. https://www.youtube.com/watch?v=zkiWD3oa37s
24. Walker, T. (n.d.). *Alarming number of educators may soon leave the profession | NEA.* https://www.nea.org/advocating-for-change/new-from-nea/survey-alarming-number-educators-may-soon-leave-profession#:~:text=A%20staggering%2055%20percent%20of,its%20members%20released%20on%20Tuesday.
25. Blad, E. (2023, July 19). Could principal apprenticeships expand the pipeline of school leaders? *Education Week.* https://www.edweek.org/leadership/could-principal-apprenticeships-expand-the-pipeline-of-school-leaders/2023/07#:~:text=About%20half%20of%20school%20leaders,a%20career%20change%20or%20retirement
26. Gross, J. A. (2016, October 28). *5 Whys example: The truth behind a monumental mystery.* The KaiZone. https://thekaizone.com/2014/08/5-whys-folklore-the-truth-behind-a-monumental-mystery/
27. *Biology and Control of Non-Biting Aquatic Midges | NC State Extension Publications.* (n.d.). https://content.ces.ncsu.edu/biology-and-control-of-non-biting-aquatic-midges
28. Plotinsky, M. (2021). *Three key ways to beat decision fatigue.* Education World. Retrieved June 30, 2024, from https://www.educationworld.com/teachers/three-key-ways-beat-decision-fatigue#:~:text=

29. Iyengar, S. S., & Lepper, M. R. (2000). When choice is demotivating: Can one desire too much of a good thing? *Journal of Personality and Social Psychology, 79*(6), 995–1006. https://doi.org/10.1037/0022-3514.79.6.995
30. Kahney, L. (2014). *Jony Ive: The Genius Behind Apple's Greatest Products.* Penguin.
31. Barkman, R. (2021, May 19). *Why the human brain is so good at detecting patterns.* Psychology Today. Retrieved June 29, 2024, from https://www.psychologytoday.com/us/blog/singular-perspective/202105/why-the-human-brain-is-so-good-detecting-patterns
32. *Top lifetime Grosses - Box office mojo.* (n.d.). Box Office Mojo. https://www.boxofficemojo.com/chart/top_lifetime_gross/?area=XWW
33. *What is the most successful Hollywood movie of all time?* (2023, May 25). Information Is Beautiful. Retrieved June 29, 2024, from https://informationisbeautiful.net/visualizations/what-is-the-most-successful-hollywood-movie-of-all-time/
34. Crosbie, E. (2023, September 8). 12 interesting things you probably didn't know about the "My Big Fat Greek Wedding" movies. *Business Insider.* https://www.insider.com/my-big-fat-greek-wedding-fun-facts-trivia-2023-9#john-corbett-was-offered-the-role-of-ian-without-an-audition-4
35. Bove, K. (2023, September 11). How much Nia Vardalos was paid for all 3 my big fat Greek wedding movies. *ScreenRant.* https://screenrant.com/my-big-fat-greek-wedding-nia-vardalos-salary-pay/#:~:text=Summary,dollars%20from%20all%20three%20movies.
36. Floman, J. L., Ponnock, A., Jain, J., & Brackett, M. A. (2024). Emotionally intelligent school leadership predicts educator well-being before and during a crisis. *Frontiers in Psychology, 14.* https://doi.org/10.3389/fpsyg.2023.1159382
37. Gaines, J., PhD. (2024, July 15). *What is emotional contagion theory? (Definition & examples).* PositivePsychology.com.

Chapter 2

38. Clark, S. R. (2023, December 13). Hawaii residents continue to recover from fire, find hope during Christmas season - The Baptist Paper. *The Baptist Paper.* https://thebaptistpaper.org/hawaii-residents-continue-to-recover-from-fire-find-hope-during-christmas-season/

NOTES

39. *Dan Barreiro | iHeart.* (n.d.). iHeart. https://www.iheart.com/podcast/462-dan-barreiro-26981004/

40. Nelson, K. (2023, September 24). *Maui's 150-year-old Banyan tree is growing leaves after being charred by the wildfires.* CNN. Retrieved June 29, 2024, from https://www.cnn.com/2023/09/24/us/lahaina-banyan-tree-wildfires-recovery/index.html

41. Staff, H. (2023, August 25). TIMELINE: This is how the Lahaina disaster unfolded, hour by hour. *https://www.hawaiinewsnow.com.* https://www.hawaiinewsnow.com/2023/08/19/timeline-look-days-events-that-led-up-devastating-lahaina-wildfire/

42. Mason, T. B., Smith, K. E., Engwall, A., Lass, A., Mead, M., Sorby, M., Bjorlie, K., Strauman, T. J., & Wonderlich, S. (2019). Self-discrepancy theory as a transdiagnostic framework: A meta-analysis of self-discrepancy and psychopathology. *Psychological Bulletin, 145*(4), 372–389. https://doi.org/10.1037/bul0000186

43. Lieberman, M. (2024, April 17). *Should leaders focus on results, or on people?* Harvard Business Review. https://hbr.org/2013/12/should-leaders-focus-on-results-or-on-people#:~:text=In%202009%2C%20James%20Zenger%20published,results%20focus%20and%20social%20skill

44. Rock, D. (2013, October 31). *Find out how many leaders are both goal and people focused.* Psychology Today. Retrieved June 30, 2024, from https://www.psychologytoday.com/us/blog/your-brain-at-work/201310/find-out-how-many-leaders-are-both-goal-and-people-focused

45. Harper, A. (2022). *Write a Must-Read: Craft a Book That Changes Lives—Including Your Own.* Page Two.

46. *Biography: Sojourner Truth.* (n.d.). Biography: Sojourner Truth. https://www.womenshistory.org/education-resources/biographies/sojourner-truth

47. Wikipedia contributors. (2024, June 20). *Sojourner Truth.* Wikipedia. https://en.wikipedia.org/wiki/Sojourner_Truth

48. Crum, A. (2018, February 9). *Stress can be a good thing if you know how to use it.* Harvard Business Review. https://hbr.org/2015/09/stress-can-be-a-good-thing-if-you-know-how-to-use-it

49. Sakaj, E. (2023, May 2). *Understanding Blame Culture- What is neuroscience bringing up, and how to navigate it?* https://www.linkedin.com/pulse/understanding-blame-culture-what-neuroscience-bringing-eleni-sakaj

50. Timms, M. (2022, February 11). *Blame culture is toxic. Here's how to stop it*. Harvard Business Review. https://hbr.org/2022/02/blame-culture-is-toxic-heres-how-to-stop-it#:~:text=A%20study%20shows%20that%20the%20brain%20responds%20more,criticism%20or%20stonewalling%2C%20the%20most%20lethal%20is%20blame
51. *Passing the buck: Blaming others is contagious*. (2010, January 19). NBC News. https://www.nbcnews.com/health/health-news/passing-buck-blaming-others-contagious-flna1c9441046
52. Kam JWY, Wan-Sai-Cheong L, Zuk AAO, Mehta A, Dixon ML, Gross JJ. A brief reappraisal intervention leads to durable affective benefits. Emotion. 2024 Jun 20. doi: 10.1037/emo0001391. Epub ahead of print. PMID: 38900559.
53. Lcsw, A. M. (2023, May 10). *How cognitive reframing works*. Verywell Mind. https://www.verywellmind.com/reframing-defined-2610419
54. Gladwell, M. (2018, August 1). *Malcolm Gladwell teaches writing*. MasterClass. https://www.masterclass.com/classes/malcolm-gladwell-teaches-writing
55. Tenney, M., Tenney, M., Tenney, M., & Tenney, M. (2023, December 4). *What is a toxic workplace culture?* Business Leadership Today - the Resource for Leaders Working to Build and Sustain World-class Teams and Organizations in Today's Business Environment. https://businessleadershiptoday.com/what-is-a-toxic-culture/#:~:text=A%20toxic%20culture%20is%20a,and%20even%20leave%20the%20organization.
56. *The Slippery-Slope effect: Minor misdeeds lead to major ones*. (n.d.). Association for Psychological Science - APS. https://www.psychologicalscience.org/news/minds-business/the-slippery-slope-effect-minor-misdeeds-lead-to-major-ones.html

Chapter 3

57. Harvardgazette, & Harvardgazette. (2019, May 2). *Wandering mind not a happy mind*. Harvard Gazette. https://news.harvard.edu/gazette/story/2010/11/wandering-mind-not-a-happy-mind/
58. Nast, C. (2016, March 13). Health myth: Do men really think about sex every 7 seconds? GQ. https://www.gq.com/story/health-myth-does-the-average-man-really-think-about-sex-every-7-seconds

NOTES

59. Raypole, C. (2022b, February 28). *How many thoughts do you have each day? and other things to think about*. Healthline. https://www.healthline.com/health/how-many-thoughts-per-day#thoughts-per-day
60. Healthy Brains by Cleveland Clinic. (2020, May 11). *Brain Facts - Healthy brains by Cleveland Clinic*. https://healthybrains.org/brain-facts/
61. Movement, M. (2018, January 5). How changing this one habit changed my life - manifest movement - medium. *Medium*. https://medium.com/@hellomanifestapp/how-changing-this-one-habit-changed-my-life-7e5092b1ef5d
62. Kauflin, J. (2021, June 29). Only 15% of people are Self-Aware -- Here's How to change. *Forbes*. https://www.forbes.com/sites/jeffkauflin/2017/05/10/only-15-of-people-are-self-aware-heres-how-to-change/
63. Eurich, T. (2023, April 6). *What Self-Awareness really is (and how to cultivate it)*. Harvard Business Review. https://hbr.org/2018/01/what-self-awareness-really-is-and-how-to-cultivate-it
64. Wikipedia contributors. (2024b, June 28). *SpaceX*. Wikipedia. https://en.wikipedia.org/wiki/SpaceX
65. *SpaceX*. (n.d.). SpaceX. https://www.spacex.com/vehicles/falcon-9/
66. MarketScreener. (2023, December 13). Musk's SpaceX value jumps closer to $180 billion in tender offer - Bloomberg News. *MarketScreener*. https://www.marketscreener.com/business-leaders/ELON-MUSK-1364/news/Musk-s-SpaceX-value-jumps-closer-to-180-billion-in-tender-offer-Bloomberg-News-45555374/#google_vignette
67. *How far away is the moon? | NASA Space Place – NASA Science for Kids*. (n.d.). https://spaceplace.nasa.gov/moon-distance/en/
68. NASA. (2024, August 1). *Hazard: distance from Earth - NASA*. https://www.nasa.gov/hrp/hazard-distance-from-earth/
69. Iyengar, S. S., & Lepper, M. R. (2000). When choice is demotivating: Can one desire too much of a good thing? *Journal of Personality and Social Psychology, 79*(6), 995–1006. https://doi.org/10.1037/0022-3514.79.6.995
70. Dweck, C. S. (2007). *Mindset: The New Psychology of Success*. Ballantine Books.
71. Dweck, C. (2024, April 2). Carol Dweck revisits the "Growth Mindset" (Opinion). *Education Week*. https://www.edweek.org/leadership/opinion-carol-dweck-revisits-the-growth-mindset/2015/09
72. Kate Anderson. (2017, April 19). *False growth Mindset - Carol Dweck* [Video]. YouTube. https://www.youtube.com/watch?v=6WbqxKUS9eQ

73. Killian, S. (2021, September 27). *False growth mindset explained - Evidence-Based teaching*. Evidence-Based Teaching. https://www.evidencebasedteaching.org.au/false-growth-mindset-explained/
74. Sturm, M. (2018, April 19). The mother of all biases: the action bias and the power of restraint. *Medium*. https://medium.com/personal-growth/the-mother-of-all-biases-the-action-bias-and-the-power-of-restraint-e3ae31b25247
75. Lester, T. L. (2009, July 13). How much time do you spend deciding what to wear? (You'll never believe what's average!). *Glamour*. https://www.glamour.com/story/how-much-time-do-you-spend-dec
76. Wall, M. (2014, February 21). How does the Curiosity Mars rover preserve its wheels? By driving backward, of course. *The Christian Science Monitor*. https://www.csmonitor.com/Science/2014/0221/How-does-the-Curiosity-Mars-rover-preserve-its-wheels-By-driving-backward-of-course
77. Wall, M. (2019, February 14). How NASA's Opportunity Mars Rover lived so long. *Space.com*. https://www.space.com/opportunity-mars-rover-long-life.html
78. Burns, S. (2023, May 30). Different types of mindsets - new trader U. *New Trader U*. https://www.newtraderu.com/2023/05/21/different-types-of-mindsets/
79. Spacey, J. (2022, August 3). *110 Types of Mindset*. Simplicable. https://simplicable.com/philosophy/mindset-types#google_vignette
80. Mcleod, S., PhD. (2023). What is cognitive dissonance Theory? *Simply Psychology*. https://www.simplypsychology.org/cognitive-dissonance.html
81. Citing women's rights, chess champ skips title defense in Saudi Arabia. (2018, January 11). *GBH*. https://www.wgbh.org/news/2018-01-11/citing-womens-rights-chess-champ-skips-title-defense-in-saudi-arabia
82. *Why is a Triangle a Strong Shape?* (2020, August 17). Let's Talk Science. https://letstalkscience.ca/educational-resources/backgrounders/why-a-triangle-a-strong-shape
83. *Chess 101: What is a poisoned pawn?* (2022, September 2). MasterClass. Retrieved June 29, 2024, from https://www.masterclass.com/articles/chess-101-what-is-a-poisoned-pawn-learn-what-makes-the-poisoned-pawn-so-tricky-in-chess-and-a-step-by-step-guide-to-using-poisoned-pawn-in-the-najdorf-variation#4ApJmWGnGGisp49xVlYVqD
84. Timms, M. (2022b, February 11). *Blame culture is toxic. Here's how to stop it*. Harvard Business Review. https://hbr.org/2022/02/

blame-culture-is-toxic-heres-how-to-stop-it#:~:text=A%20study%20 shows%20that%20the%20brain%20responds%20more,criticism%20 or%20stonewalling%2C%20the%20most%20lethal%20is%20blame
85. *NASA's Airless Tire Technology Rethinks Rover Tire Design with Earth Applications | T2 Portal.* (n.d.). https://technology.nasa.gov/page/nasas-airless-tire-technology-re
86. Welch, N. (2023, July 26). The little tires that could…go to Mars - NASA. NASA. https://www.nasa.gov/solar-system/the-little-tires-that-could-go-to-mars/

Chapter 4

87. Reader, H. (2023, February 20). *21 Funniest Cultural Misunderstandings & Miscommunications - Hasty Reader.* Hasty Reader. https://hastyreader.com/misunderstanding/
88. McCusker, B. (2024, February 15). *The 13 presidents with the highest IQ scores.* The Healthy. https://www.rd.com/list/presidents-with-the-highest-iq-scores/
89. Nannestad, C. (2023, December 14). *10 surprising facts you didn't know about Jimmy Carter.* Readers Digest. https://www.rd.com/list/jimmy-carter-presidency/
90. Benner, M., & Quirk, A. (2020, February 20). *One size does not fit all: Analyzing different approaches to Family-School communication.* Cap20. Retrieved August 13, 2024, from https://www.americanprogress.org/article/one-size-not-fit/
91. *Attunement – Being aware and responsive to emotions.* (n.d.). https://education.gov.scot/media/qobanx4l/information-note-attunement.pdf
92. Lisitsa, E. (2024, June 25). *Emotional attunement.* The Gottman Institute. https://www.gottman.com/blog/self-care-emotional-attunement/
93. Kolber, A. (2020). *Try softer.* Tyndale House Publishers, Inc.
94. *The psychology behind saying hurtful things we don't mean.* (n.d.). The Swaddle. https://www.theswaddle.com/the-psychology-behind-saying-hurtful-things-we-dont-mean
95. Wright, K. (2008, May 1). *Dare to be yourself.* Psychology Today. https://www.psychologytoday.com/us/articles/200805/dare-be-yourself

96. Reviewed by Staff. (n.d.). *Authenticity.* Psychology Today. Retrieved June 30, 2024, from https://www.psychologytoday.com/us/basics/authenticity#:~:text=A%20recent%20study%20finds%20that,are%20some%20of%20the%20implications.&text=Sometimes%20the%20greatest%20act%20of,telling%20someone%20a%20hard%20truth.
97. Bloom, C., & Bloom, L. (2019, September 12). *Self-trust and how to build it.* Psychology Today. https://www.psychologytoday.com/au/blog/stronger-the-broken-places/201909/self-trust-and-how-build-it#:~:text=Self%2Dtrust%20is%20not%20trusting,the%20outcome%20of%20your%20efforts.
98. Andrés. (2024, March 20). *Three stories that demonstrate how your communication skills can change your life.* Astrolab. Storytelling, Innovation Culture and Learning Experiences. https://www.astrolab.mx/en/three-stories-that-demonstrate-how-your-communication-skills-can-change-your-life/
99. Staff, K. a. W. (2020, October 13). *Better communication through neuroscience.* Knowledge at Wharton. https://knowledge.wharton.upenn.edu/article/better-communication-neuroscience/
100. Mulvaney, K. (2023, May 16). The search for the loneliest whale in the world. *The Guardian.* https://www.theguardian.com/environment/2021/jul/13/loneliest-whale-in-the-world-search

Chapter 5

101. McCarthy, J. (2017, December 26). A lifetime of planting trees on a remote river island: Meet India's forest man. *NPR.* https://www.npr.org/sections/parallels/2017/12/26/572421590/hed-take-his-own-life-before-killing-a-tree-meet-india-s-forest-man
102. *Profile of Martha's Vineyard.* (n.d.). Martha's Vinyard Commission. Retrieved June 30, 2024, from https://www.mvcommission.org/profile-marthas-vineyard#:~:text=Martha's%20Vineyard%20is%20a%20100,the%20coast%20of%20Cape%20Cod.
103. Hutchinson, S. (2023, June 29). 25 Incisive Facts about "Jaws." *Mental Floss.* https://www.mentalfloss.com/article/64548/25-incisive-facts-about-jaws
104. *AFI's 100 YEARS...100 HEROES & VILLAINS.* (n.d.). American Film Institute. https://www.afi.com/afis-100-years-100-heroes-villians/

NOTES

105. Jaws, D. (2022, June 20). *When do we first see the shark in Jaws?* — *The Daily Jaws*. The Daily Jaws. https://thedailyjaws.com/blog/when-do-we-first-see-the-shark-in-jaws
106. Metcalfe, T. (2019, June 24). *Back to the Stone Age: 17 key milestones in Paleolithic life*. livescience.com. https://www.livescience.com/65775-stone-age-milestones-photos.html
107. Hanson, R. (2019, February 19). *Common ground*. Psychology Today. https://www.psychologytoday.com/us/blog/your-wise-brain/201902/common-ground?amp
108. Fast, N. J., Heath, C., University of Chicago, Stanford University, & Wu, G. (2009). Common Ground and Cultural prominence: How conversation Reinforces culture. In *PSYCHOLOGICAL SCIENCE* (No. 7; Vol. 20, p. 904). https://msbfile03.usc.edu/digitalmeasures/nathanaf/intellcont/Common_ground_and_cultural_prominence-1.pdf
109. Petriello, M. (2023, February 24). *Lugo spins a Statcast curveball record*. *MLB.com*. https://www.mlb.com/news/seth-lugo-sets-statcast-curveball-spin-record-c198720622
110. McRaney, D. (2017, May 1). *YANSS 093 – The neuroscience of changing your mind*. You Are Not so Smart. https://youarenotsosmart.com/2017/01/13/yanss-093-the-neuroscience-of-changing-your-mind/
111. *You're not going to believe what I'm about to tell you*. (n.d.). The Oatmeal. https://theoatmeal.com/comics/believe
112. Shah, A. (2020, January 17). *How do Sea Stars move without a brain?* Phys Org. https://phys.org/news/2020-01-sea-stars-brain-impact-robotics.html
113. *2024 Global Culture Report*. (2024). O.C. Tanner Institute. Retrieved June 30, 2024, from https://res.cloudinary.com/oct-corp/image/private/s--XG19pHOM--/v1693428631/website/OCTanner-2024-Global-Culture-Report.pdf
114. Amabile, T. M. (2020, May 6). *The power of small wins*. Harvard Business Review. https://hbr.org/2011/05/the-power-of-small-wins
115. Gammon, K. (2023, December 6). *Peace-building in War: Psychologist and Practicing mediator Olga Maria Klimecki-Lenz on Strategies for Manipulating Emotion in Mediation*. Nautilus. https://nautil.us/what-gets-enemies-to-negotiate-460629/?_sp=b9180a08-89b0-4d2f-8d81-df2a92589048.1716156565343

116. Greenspan, J., & Greenspan, J. (2023, November 1). *How Jimmy Carter brokered a Hard-Won peace deal between Israel and Egypt.* HISTORY. https://www.history.com/news/jimmy-carter-camp-david-accords-egypt-israel

Chapter 6

117. *How fast do you fall?* (n.d.). https://skydivenorthwest.co.uk/about-skydiving/how-fast-do-you-fall/#:~:text=It%20takes%20very%20roughly%2010,roughly%2060%20seconds%20of%20freefall.%20https://www.history.com/topics/black-history/sojourner-truth
118. Logue, I. (2024, June 13). TRANSCRIPT: Tom Brady's Hall of Fame Induction Speech. *PatsFans.com.* https://www.patsfans.com/patriots/blog/2024/06/12/transcript-tom-bradys-hall-of-fame-induction-speech/
119. Solis-Moreira, J. (2024, February 20). How long does it really take to form a habit? *Scientific American.* https://www.scientificamerican.com/article/how-long-does-it-really-take-to-form-a-habit/
120. Lally, P., Van Jaarsveld, C. H. M., Potts, H. W. W., & Wardle, J. (2009). How are habits formed: Modelling habit formation in the real world. *European Journal of Social Psychology, 40*(6), 998–1009. https://doi.org/10.1002/ejsp.674
121. Krysti (Lan Chi) Vo, MD. (2024, January 15). The simple science of habit stacking | Krysti VO MD, Psychiatric and Behavioral Therapy. *Krysti Vo, MD › Vo.Care Psychiatry and Behavioral Therapy.* https://vo.care/the-simple-science-of-habit-stacking/#:~:text=TL%3BDR%20We%20explore%20the,natural%20inclination%20to%20automate%20tasks.
122. Lima, J. K. (2024). *Worthy: How to Believe You are enough and Transform Your Life - by Jamie Kern Lima Pre-Order.* Hay House, Inc.
123. Sorvino, C. (2017, May 23). *How Jamie Kern Lima built IT cosmetics into a $1.2 billion business.* Forbes. https://www.forbes.com/sites/chloesorvino/2017/05/17/jamie-kern-lima-loreal-beauty-it-cosmetics/
124. Nikolopoulou, K. (2023, May 30). *False dilemma fallacy.* Scribbr. https://www.scribbr.com/fallacies/false-dilemma-fallacy/
125. *What the Stockdale Paradox tells us about crisis leadership.* (2020, August 17). HBS Working Knowledge. https://hbswk.hbs.edu/item/what-the-stockdale-paradox-tells-us-about-crisis-leadership

NOTES

126. Najarro, I. (2022, April 26). Here's how many hours a week teachers work. *Education Week.* https://www.edweek.org/teaching-learning/heres-how-many-hours-a-week-teachers-work/2022/04
127. Jackson, B. (2023, May 18). *Astro for kids: How many stars are there in space?* Astronomy Magazine. https://www.astronomy.com/science/astro-for-kids-how-many-stars-are-there-in-space/
128. *How many constellations are there? – Constellation guide.* (n.d.). https://www.constellation-guide.com/what-is-a-constellation/how-many-constellations-are-there/
129. Donohoo, J., Katz, S., & Learning Forward. (2017). WHEN TEACHERS BELIEVE, STUDENTS ACHIEVE: COLLABORATIVE INQUIRY BUILDS TEACHER EFFICACY FOR BETTER STUDENT OUTCOMES. *The Learning Professional,* 6, 21–23. https://learningforward.org/wp-content/uploads/2017/12/when-teachers-believe-students-achieve.pdf
130. Hattie, J. (2023). *Visible Learning: the sequel: A Synthesis of Over 2,100 Meta-Analyses Relating to Achievement.* Routledge.
131. *The power of collective efficacy.* (2021, November 1). ASCD. https://www.ascd.org/el/articles/the-power-of-collective-efficacy
132. *Lippert.* (n.d.). https://corporate.lippert.com/about
133. Kruse, K. (2023, September 12). Leadership development is the lever for a thriving culture. *Forbes.* https://www.forbes.com/sites/kevinkruse/2023/09/07/at-lippert-leadership-development-is-the-lever-for-a-thriving-culture/
134. How do Skydivers land accurately? (2017, May 22). *Jumptown.* https://www.jumptown.com/blog/how-do-skydivers-land-accurately

Chapter 7

135. Snapes, L. (2022, February 11). Rick Rubin: Def Jam founder and producer announces debut book. *The Guardian.* https://www.theguardian.com/music/2022/feb/11/rick-rubin-def-jam-founder-producer-debut-book
136. *Rick Rubin - purple MAGAZINE.* (2021, March 9). Purple. https://purple.fr/magazine/fw-2010-issue-14/rick-rubin/#:~:text=RICK%20RUBIN%20E2%80%93%20It's%20funny%20E2%80%94%20the,strong%20foundation%20for%20a%20building.

137. Baier, D. (2024, August 20). *District professional learning session.* Reference to classroom poster.
138. Key-notes. (2019, December 28). *What is sympathetic resonance?* [Video]. YouTube. https://www.youtube.com/watch?v=c2VHVjHxvq0
139. Wikipedia contributors. (2024a, May 27). *Sympathetic resonance.* Wikipedia. https://en.wikipedia.org/wiki/Sympathetic_resonance#:~:text=The%20classic%20example%20is%20demonstrated,no%20physical%20contact%20between%20them.
140. Pultarova, T., Howell, E., Dobrijevic, D., & Mann, A. (2024, May 30). *Starlink satellites: Facts, tracking and impact on astronomy.* Space.com. https://www.space.com/spacex-starlink-satellites.html

Integrity of Research and Writing

I attempted to make the sources and studies I referenced throughout this book very clear. If you're unsure of whether a study, data point, or historical story is original, assume credit should be given to the previously cited source.

About the Author

Dr. Brad Gustafson is an award-winning principal, best-selling author, and lover of life. He understands how challenging it can be to lead transformational change, make a difference, and stay awake past 7:30 p.m. on Friday night. When he's not reading or writing, Brad can be found fishing, apple farming, and laughing with some of his favorite people: his wife and their three kids.

Brad has served as a national advisor with Future Ready Schools, Scholastic Principal Advisory Board, and educational technology consultant over the years. He's also authored several books including, *Renegade Leadership*, *Reclaiming Our Calling*, and *The 6 Literacy Levers*. He co-hosts a weekly web series and is actively engaged with school leaders across the country.

Brad started his career as an elementary teacher, varsity boys soccer coach, and student council advisor. He's been a principal for more than fifteen years and was recognized as Minnesota's Principal of the Year in 2016. He was also named a "20 to Watch" by the National School Boards Association. Brad's team has also been recognized with a Digital Innovation in Learning Award (DILA) from EdSurge and Digital Promise, and a Local Government Innovation Award from the Humphrey School of Public Affairs at the University of Minnesota.

If you or your organization would like to connect with Brad for support with your speaking needs, book study, or just to talk about Jesus, you can contact him through his website (BradGustafson.com) or on the various social media channels he dabbles with.

More from ConnectEDD Publishing

Since 2015, ConnectEDD has worked to transform education by empowering educators to become better-equipped to teach, learn, and lead. What started as a small company designed to provide professional learning events for educators has grown to include a variety of services to help educators and administrators address essential challenges. ConnectEDD offers instructional and leadership coaching, professional development workshops focusing on a variety of educational topics, a roster of nationally recognized educator associates who possess hands-on knowledge and experience, educational conferences custom-designed to meet the specific needs of schools, districts, and state/national organizations, and ongoing, personalized support, both virtually and onsite. In 2020, ConnectEDD expanded to include publishing services designed to provide busy educators with books and resources consisting of practical information on a wide variety of teaching, learning, and leadership topics. Please visit us online at connecteddpublishing.com or contact us at: info@connecteddpublishing.com

Recent Publications:

Live Your Excellence: Action Guide by Jimmy Casas

Culturize: Action Guide by Jimmy Casas

Daily Inspiration for Educators: Positive Thoughts for Every Day of the Year by Jimmy Casas

Eyes on Culture: Multiply Excellence in Your School by Emily Paschall

Pause. Breathe. Flourish. Living Your Best Life as an Educator by William D. Parker

L.E.A.R.N.E.R. Finding the True, Good, and Beautiful in Education by Marita Diffenbaugh

Educator Reflection Tips Volume II: Refining Our Practice by Jami Fowler-White

Handle With Care: Managing Difficult Situations in Schools with Dignity and Respect by Jimmy Casas and Joy Kelly

Disruptive Thinking: Preparing Learners for Their Future by Eric Sheninger

Permission to be Great: Increasing Engagement in Your School by Dan Butler

Daily Inspiration for Educators: Positive Thoughts for Every Day of the Year, Volume II by Jimmy Casas

The 6 Literacy Levers: Creating a Community of Readers by Brad Gustafson

The Educator's ATLAS: Your Roadmap to Engagement by Weston Kieschnick

In This Season: Words for the Heart by Todd Nesloney, LaNesha Tabb, Tanner Olson, and Alice Lee

Leading with a Humble Heart: A 40-Day Devotional for Leaders by Zac Bauermaster

MORE FROM CONNECTEDD PUBLISHING

Recalibrate the Culture: Our Why…Our Work…Our Values by Jimmy Casas

Creating Curious Classrooms: The Beauty of Questions by Emma Chiappetta

Crafting the Culture: 45 Reflections on What Matters Most by Joe Sanfelippo and Jeffrey Zoul

Improving School Mental Health: The Thriving School Community Solution by Charle Peck and Dr. Cameron Caswell

Building Authenticity: A Blueprint for the Leader Inside You by Todd Nesloney And Tyler Cook

Connecting Through Conversation: A Playbook for Talking with Kids by Erika Bare and Tiffany Burns

The Dream Factory: Designing a Purposeful Life by Mark Trumbo

Stories Behind Stances: Creating Empathy Through Hearing "The Other Side" by Chris Singleton

Happy Eyes: Becoming All Things to All People by Ryan Tillman

The Generative Age Artificial Intelligence and the Future of Education by Alana Winnick

Recalibrate the Culture: Action Guide by Jimmy Casas

Leading with PEOPLE: A Six Pillar Framework for Fruitful Leadership by Zac Bauermaster

A School Leader's Guide to Reclaiming Purpose by Frederick C. Buskey

Foundations of an Elite Culture: Building Success with High Standards and a Positive Environment by David Arencibia

Personalize: Meeting the Needs of All Learners by Eric Sheninger and Nicki Slaugh

The Five Principles of Educator Professionalism: Rebuilding Trust in Schools by Nason Lollar

Words on the Wall: Culturizing Your Classroom for Observable Impact by Jimmy Casas and Cale Birk

School of Engagement: 45 Activities to Ignite Student Learning by Jonathan Alsheimer

Intentional Instructional Moves: Strategic Steps to Accelerate Student Learning by Sherry St. Clair